FUN AND PROFIT
IN STAMP COLLECTING

*May you have the fun —
and the profit, too!*

Herman Herst, Jr.

FUN AND PROFIT
IN STAMP COLLECTING

Revised Edition

by HERMAN HERST, Jr.

HAWTHORN BOOKS, INC.
Publishers/*New York*

To all those who collect
stamps for their prime reward,
pleasure.

FUN AND PROFIT IN STAMP COLLECTING
Revised Edition

Library of Congress Catalog Card Number: 75–20913

ISBN: 0-8015-2851-8

2 3 4 5 6 7 8 9 10

CONTENTS

FOREWORD

This book is definitely not titled "How to Make Money in Stamps." Money has been made in stamps, but we would not be so naïve as to suggest that it can be done simply by reading a book. No book can be a substitute for the time, knowledge, and experience that one needs to emerge from the hobby of philately not only with a greater share of pleasure, but with a greater measure of investment increment as well.

It is sadly ironic that the philatelic speculator who enters the hobby with the cold-blooded aim of making money seldom does. It is equally ironic that a collector whose principal desire is the myriad of advantages philately offers, other than the financial, often emerges with a greater nest egg than the one with which he started.

We hope in the pages to follow to explain why this is so, and why invariably the ones who wash their hands of stamp collecting, saying, "It's nothing but a racket," have only themselves to blame.

This book will not tell anyone how to make money in stamps, but it will be difficult for anyone reading it, and profiting by its advice, suggestions, and help, to lose money on his "investment." The word is in quotes, for by definition the purchase of stamps cannot be regarded as an investment. An investment is a speculation that pays dividends all the while the principal remains relatively secure. The dividends that philately pays are many, but they are not of the financial variety.

"Speculation," of course, is a naughty word, especially in philately, but every purchase is a speculation. When one buys a car, in choosing the make of car he is speculating on his chances of obtaining trouble-free performance. When one buys insurance, he is speculating—in fact, wagering—with the insurance company on his chances of living out the period for which the insurance is in force.

When a collector buys a stamp, there are many things that enter into the price. The proportions of each segment of the collector's dollar will vary with the individual. The topical collector who has sought and finally obtained the only stamp that he needed picturing geysers will allot much more of the cost to satisfaction and the end of the chase than will one who has vowed to obtain 100 White Plains souvenir sheets, and finally achieves the goal.

There is nothing wrong in seeking full value for what one spends, whether it is in stamps or any other commodity. There is nothing wrong in spending a dollar for something worth perhaps a dime if one is aware of the fact, and if one can satisfy himself that the pride of possession which he now assumes is worth the other ninety cents. This may be the end of a long and thus far fruitless pursuit; it may be in the esteem in which he thinks he will be held by his friends, for having achieved his goal; it may even be in the pleasant future prospects of admiring a long-sought stamp for its beauty, for its condition, or for its uniqueness.

This book presupposes one very important thing: that the reader is possessed of at least normal intelligence, and that he knows that there is no substitute for knowledge. There is no ready-made formula, at any price, that will guarantee anyone a profitable venture into philately if the financial aims are paramount.

On the other hand, we defy any person of better-than-average intelligence to read this book and not find himself better informed when he has finished it, and far more likely to emerge with security of capital, and perhaps a neat financial profit, than one who has not.

There are a few truths which must be considered before we get down to specifics. Some of them may be bitter pills to swallow. There will be many who in good faith will question them. There will be others who may well claim that we have not stressed them sufficiently. As far as we are concerned, we regard them as gospel. Whether or not one agrees, let us consider them.

The person buying stamps solely to make money on them will probably lose on them. It goes without saying that not all professional stamp dealers are successful. It has been said that there is no business in which a smaller percentage of those involved achieve a considerable measure of success. There are many who make a living; there are many who are quite comfortable. But the number driving Cadillacs, the number with summer homes in the country is definitely limited. In our thirty years as a professional we have yet to encounter one professional with a yacht.

This is a fact which must be reckoned with. True, we seldom hear of a bankruptcy in the stamp field. This is perhaps why so many look upon the field as one in which mere entrance to it is a gold-plated guarantee of success. But if one picks up a stamp magazine of even five years ago, and reads the advertisements, the first thing that will strike him will be the names of those then advertising who are no longer in the field.

They did not go bankrupt, to be sure. Those who were roofers are now back putting shingles on houses. Those who were taxi drivers are now back behind the wheel. Those who were clerks in stores are back behind the counter. Many of these found the stamp business a great success as long as they had their collections to sell, but when their principal stock in trade vanished, so did their business. For there are few commodities in the business world akin to stamps. One may open a shoe store, and if he is fortunate enough to merit considerable patronage, he will sell a great many shoes. With empty shelves, a mere phone call will bring a new supply, and he can continue his merry way, selling what he has and replacing what he sells. The druggest, the grocer, the baker is in the same position. The supply can be found with ease to meet the demand.

It is not so with stamps. With the exception of new issues (which field has its own laws, and which will be covered later) there is only one source for stamps: the collector. The stamps in the hands of dealers represent only the floating supply; at all times by far the greater number of stamps of any issue are in collections, and usually they are not for sale. This is an awkward situation. The dealer seeking to replenish his stock can only turn to the very people to whom he has sold his stamps, and, in most cases, they are reluctant to sell. Only when death, illness, or loss of interest requires it does a collection come on the market, and the dealer seeking stock then must compete not only with fellow dealers needing merchandise perhaps more urgently than he does, but with the ultimate retail customers as well. It is the dream of every collector with a collection to sell that he may sell it to another collector in order to obtain a higher price for it. (This is a fallacy, which will be dealt with later.)

There is another aphorism which may be questioned by some but which to us seems absolutely elementary.

The collector is buying at retail, and when he sells, he perforce sells at wholesale. Given a market that is static—and this can happen in philately—the difference between retail and wholesale will be the precise degree of his loss. And given a declining market, and this can happen in philately, the degree of his loss will be that much greater.

But it is the stamps that will increase in price which the collector wishes to buy, just as in real estate, stocks, and bonds, or any other similar field, it is the things which will go up which are to be desired. Life would be far simpler if there were a means of readily identifying these before purchase. There is not. Again we must face the fact that there are many dealers who do have the facilities to buy at wholesale and the same opportunity to sell at retail as anyone else, and success is not assured to them either.

The stamp field is unique in another way. The professionals are seldom reluctant to share their experience with their customers. A lawyer's client might think twice about cold-bloodedly asking the advice of his attorney without expecting a bill. The patient visiting a doctor is prepared for the bill he will receive. But we have had customers come to us to ask the name of a client to whom they might sell a stamp they have for sale, or to suggest a dealer from whom they might buy a certain stamp at less than the normal price ... and some of these have appeared shocked when told nicely that the request is a bit bizarre.

Nevertheless, good advice, as a general rule is available for the asking from your favorite dealer. Advice is a freely given commodity in philately. It is not always good advice. Of necessity, it is sometimes tinged with the profit motive, for it will take a dealer of strong moral fortitude to advise against the purchase of a stamp that the customer wishes to buy and which the dealer has to sell.

But, as a general rule, good advice is available from a relatively successful, well-established dealer. However, the mere fact that a professional is giving the advice does not necessarily make it good advice. We would be more inclined to accept the advice from a dealer of repute who has himself had considerable experience in the field than from a Johnny-come-lately part-time dealer whose philatelic knowledge may not even equal that of the one asking the question.

One would think that this is elementary, but the number of collectors who have come to us with pearls of wisdom they have gleaned from curbstone dealers is incredibly large. Even more astounding than the small number of collectors willing to take good advice is the large number of those who accept and act upon bad advice, simply because it is what they want to hear.

And so, to repeat, this book presupposes a reasonable amount of intelligence on the part of the reader. If he does not have it, what is to follow is just so much wasted ink, paper, and time.

PREFACE

Great as the need for philatelic expertise was in 1962, when the first edition of *Fun and Profit* appeared, it is much increased today. Amateur stamp collecting—fast becoming the nation's number one hobby—has been contaminated by opportunists and non-philatelists. They advertise flashy stamps and expensively produced covers, hoping that the collector will be induced to buy. The amateur's only protection against this unwise speculation is philatelic knowledge, which the ethical stamp dealer can provide. Long after the mail-order gift house and the fly-by-night dealer have gone out of business or invested in tulip bulbs, fancy whiskey bottles, or calendar plates, the reputable dealer will be ready to serve the collector.

The value of the Market Guide at the back of this book cannot be overemphasized, especially for collectors seeking financial dividends. The section has been completely rewritten in light of today's market. We can only hope that the current prophecies will prove as clairvoyant as were those printed in the first edition's guide. Readers are reminded that the text of this book was written in 1962, and where catalog or market prices are given, they refer to the prices that were in effect at that time.

1. *Cheap stamps never become rare.* Cheap stamps may become popular. Cheap stamps may increase considerably in value, and often do. Barring an unforeseen calamity, such as the destruction of an issue overnight, they never become scarce.

Cheapness in a stamp is due solely to availability, and with the factor of availability, there can be no factor of scarcity.

The stamps of the remote islands of Tristan da Cunha were not necessarily plentiful, nor were they particularly popular. One could obtain them from these remote islands, but because of irregular and uncertain mail service, few imported them. The Crown agents for the Colonies obligingly maintained an office in London for their sale at face value to dealers, and dealers regularly offered them for sale at a very slight advance over their face value. There was no great demand for them, since it has always been the custom of collectors to neglect the purchase of those issues that would seem to be available indefinitely.

Of course, no one could foresee that a volcanic explosion would render the islands uninhabitable overnight. More to the point, no one foresaw that the postal authorities, once having taken refuge on a relief vessel, would throw the entire stock of stamps overboard. And to round out the threefold series of unexpected events, no one knew that the Crown agents would

3

discontinue the sale of the stamps, once the resettlement of the islands was deemed impractical.

We have here all of the elements of a philatelic boom, and this is precisely what occurred. But it must be emphasized that the stamps of Tristan da Cunha were not cheap in the philatelic sense of being common. They were cheap because they were of relatively low face value, because they were easily obtainable, and because they were not particularly popular. The reader will grasp the point which is being made, and which will be discussed at greater length later: supply and demand work in the stamp market as in every other market.

Today the possessor of a set of the U.S. Zeppelins of 1930 is regarded by the collecting fraternity as a Croesus on a minor scale. The collector who has a set of them in blocks is perhaps the most envied member of the local club. True, all that he did to obtain them was to provide a sum of money equal to the asking price, and he automatically entered the charmed circle. But there are tens of thousands, perhaps more, who had the same opportunity, but who chose not to avail themselves of it.

For the Zeppelins in 1930, to use a trite phrase, were a drug on the market. A vast quantity of them were printed, and they were available at many post offices for a long period of time, at $4.55 per set. It was too much for many collectors, and they were passed by. When the Post Office saw that they were not selling, rather than continuing to carry them for a nonbuying public, most of the issue was destroyed. Only about 65,000 complete sets, those that had been sold up to the day of destruction, were left in existence, and the price doubled overnight.

None of these, however, were cheap stamps, but they were low in price, or relatively so, because they were easily available. So was the 50¢ Zeppelin stamp of 1933. Had collectors learned their lesson from the original Zeppelin? Apparently, they had not, for this stamp went begging for more than a year, for so long in fact that hundreds of thousands of these were similarly destroyed.

Back in the 1890s, one could buy a packet of two thousand different stamps for about two dollars. Some years back, we purchased the stock of a once prominent dealer of Toledo, Ohio. As is true with most dealers, there was a large quantity of material that had been filed away decades before, the presence of which probably had not been suspected for many years. Among these were a quantity of these packets.

While we knew better than to expect a "find," one summer day for want of something better to do, we catalogued them by the then current catalogue. The average catalogue value per stamp was slightly over three cents. (The lowest figure in the catalogue of course is two cents.)

If one were to catalogue a packet of two thousand different stamps today (still available incidentally, for about two dollars), the average catalogue value would still be a trifle over three cents per stamp. Of course, the contents of the two packets would vary considerably; there have been tens of thousands of common stamps issued in the intervening seven decades. But the important point is that in seventy years, the two thousand stamps that were common when originally assembled, are equally common today.

This is often difficult for the non-philatelist to believe. The non-collector, and even the new collector, prefers to believe that if it is old, it is rare, and that if it is rare, it is valuable. One by no means follows the other. There are any number of U.S. stamps over a century old that sell for far less than U.S. stamps issued just last year.

The first stamp in the world, the famed Penny Black of Great Britain, issued in 1840, is far from a rarity. Although because of its extreme popularity it sells for a few dollars, it is still available in large quantities. Auction sales containing not hundreds, but thousands of them, are by no means unusual. Popular it is, but a rarity it can never become; yet no stamps can boast of greater antiquity.

It is difficult for many people to accept the fact that rarity does not make for value.

The height of absurdity was the offer of an old letter we once received from a well-meaning elderly lady. She brought it in, neatly protected with tissue paper, and opening it gingerly, she told its history. It was written by her grandfather, a fine old gentleman, despite the fact that he had had no schooling; in fact, he did not learn to write until his daughter, my visitor's mother, had taught him the rudiments of writing very late in life. A subsequent fire had destroyed most of the possessions of the old man, but apparently one letter had escaped the flames ... the very one which we were having the privilege to purchase.

Undoubtedly rare the letter was, but we had to explain to the disappointed owner that it had no value. It might have had sentimental value; certainly it was an interesting item. One could linger over the illegible scrawls, the misspelled words. One could imagine the patience of the daughter, teaching her father to form each letter, to make loops in the *e*'s and to omit them from the *i*'s. And one could not question the fact that, as a philatelic item, the letter and its accompanying envelope were undoubtedly unique. Sentimentally, it could have been priceless; practically, a king's ransom added to all the gold in Fort Knox could not duplicate it, but commercially it was valueless.

In our book, *Nassau Street,* we told of the collector in Arkansas who had read that stamps were a good investment, so he decided to put a portion of his salary each week into stamps. A stationery store near his place of employment had a fine assortment of packets and sets, which were frequently changed. Faithfully and religiously, our friend spent a quarter each week for almost ten years. Each stamp he neatly mounted in a large loose-leaf album, which was soon followed by another album, and another.

At the time of his death, his philatelic expenditure had amounted to well over a thousand dollars, aside from the cost of the albums. To his wife, this was a splendid asset, and in fact, in the inventory of the estate, it was the most valuable single asset. Her consternation at being told that it was comparatively valueless can easily be imagined. Even the attorney for the estate, having spent several weeks cataloguing the collection, was shocked, for according to the catalogue, the three albums had a valuation of several thousand dollars. The principal obstacle to ready sale was the fact that the average catalogue value of each stamp was just three cents!

Most collectors know that the lowest price at which any stamp is catalogued is two cents. Even this figure is being challenged today, and in the not distant future, in all probability the minimum price will be raised to three cents. For no matter how common a stamp is, and no matter how easily obtainable it is, a stamp dealer on being asked for a single copy of it cannot justifiably be asked to sell it for less than two cents. And even at two cents, the cost of doing business being what it is today, it is doubtful whether the dealer will feel that in obtaining full catalogue value for it, he is engaging in a particularly profitable business transaction.

The packet makers and packet sellers find this situation to their liking of course, and one cannot blame them. The newer collectors are attracted to the ads offering "five hundred different all genuine postage stamps from all countries of the world cataloguing ten dollars for only twenty-five cents." To the uninitiated, it indeed seems a fantastic bargain, until one stops to think that if one gathered together five hundred of the

7

most common stamps in the world, they would still catalogue ten dollars.

Common they may be, but they are also stamps. The packet seller is quite correct when he says that though they may be cheap, the most valuable collections in the world contain them, and no collection can hope to be complete without them!

Actually, as most members of the trade know, the value of the actual stamps in a packet can be the least expensive portion of it. In a packet that sells at the five-and-ten for a dime, often the window envelope and the printing will cost two or three cents. The labor in assembling the packet is easily another cent. The profit margin of the seller is perhaps a nickel; what is left, but a cent or two, represents the cost of the stamps.

It's no wonder that the widow from Arkansas was disappointed in the offers she received on her husband's thousand-dollar investment!

There are of course many stamps reputed to be rare, when such is far from the case. More than once every collector has seen a full-page advertisement offering for sale some new-found variety, or a set of stamps, or a made-to-order flight or first-day cover with the screaming letters: *"VERY RARE."* Then often follows the explanation of its rarity, how only 100,000 were made, after which the plates were destroyed. Then comes the price: $10 each, $90 per hundred, $850 per thousand. One may assume that if he wishes to buy ten thousand examples, the price will be even further reduced. The absurdity of calling an item rare which is freely available by the thousand should be so ludicrous that the response to the advertisement might be expected to be negligible. Such is not usually the case, for the word "rare," whether its use is justified or not, carries the aura of responsibility that induces those who should know better to rush to buy.

We do not suggest that cheap stamps may never increase in

value. Theoretically, every stamp ever issued becomes scarcer with each passing day, once the supply is established. The mortality figure in stamps is high. They are, after all, delicate bits of paper, and a swarm of enemies bent on their destruction daily make the remaining ones less plentiful. Dampness, sunlight, careless handling, fire, insect pests, and outright loss all play their part. But even if half the outstanding supply of a very common stamp were to be destroyed overnight, it need not necessarily have any effect on the value of the remainder. They will remain common.

There is a factor, however, that will have an effect on the price of a relatively common stamp. It is a factor which has been mentioned before, and which will be mentioned again. It is a factor that cannot be stressed too often: demand.

One of our greatest philatelic students, Dr. Carroll Chase, devoted many years of his life to the study of what was a half century ago one of our commonest stamps, the three-cent imperforate of 1851. It was so common that twenty-five cents could buy a hundred of them; dealers bought and sold them in much larger quantities at much lower prices. Dr. Chase studied the stamps. He knew what all philatelists know: no matter how identical two stamps might appear to the untrained eye, every stamp in a sheet of stamps differed in some respect from its neighbor.

By the study of each stamp, its original position in the pane could be established beyond a doubt. This is called "plating." An almost microscopic variance on a stamp with sheet margins at the left and top would be certain to be from the upper left corner of the sheet. If one then were to find a horizontal pair, the left stamp of which bore the same characteristics (even though it may not have had the sheet margins), one now has two stamps from the original pane. A vertical strip of three, with the top stamp having been proven to be similar to one in

9

the pair would give two more positions. Eventually, after years of study of tens of thousands of stamps, one could successfully reconstruct the original layout of each of the hundred stamps.

Difficult as this process may seem, and it was difficult, it should be mentioned that on this particular stamp, there were a number of different plates engraved from which the stamps were printed. Thus, the corner stamp mentioned above could conceivably come from any of several different plates; although from the same position in the pane, it was not necessarily from the same plate. Before Dr. Chase had completed "plating" the entire issue, he had successfully identified and recorded the characteristics of thousands of stamps that up to then had appeared identical to the average collector.

Dr. Chase's findings were published in a book, which became extremely popular. This was the ultimate in philately, the study of a relatively common stamp. It was to philately what the jigsaw puzzle became to the country decades later, and the similarity to the process of reconstructing a previously united picture is a particularly apt one. And then collectors found a not surprising thing. What had been a very common and cheap stamp suddenly began to increase in price. As more and more turned to plating it, the price increase continued. Dr. Chase himself probably did not have even the cost of publishing the book returned to him, for with the thousands of illustrations required it was an expensive venture. However, what he lost in the publishing, he much more than made up for in the stamps. Possessed of many thousands of the stamps, he was able to sell those he no longer required for his study for many times the price he had paid for them.

Today the three-cent 1851 remains a very popular stamp. It catalogues at seventy cents, far, far more than it did when Dr. Chase started his studies. Without question, it is the most sought-after stamp in the world, since anyone requiring it for plating needs not a single specimen, but each of the thousands of different varieties that, when properly assembled, make up the complete plating.

Withal, it is a common stamp, and withal, it can never become rare. Cheap stamps never become rare.

2. *Demand is a more important factor than supply.* Some sixteen years ago, when we moved our business from the metropolis to rural Shrub Oak, we started a collection of postal history of the area. The Shrub Oak post office itself had a long and varied history; the town goes back to long before Revolutionary days, and in the local graveyard are many of its former citizens who died owing their allegiance to King George III.

Apparently no one had ever before conceived the idea of collecting philatelic souvenirs of Shrub Oak's early days, and as news spread in the trade, many of our friends were kind enough to send us early items which we were happy to add to the collection.

On several occasions, as news of the collection's existence spread, we were asked to display it, to talk upon it, or to write articles on it. This we were very happy to do, for such a program would often bring to light other items which we would be happy to purchase for the collection.

The local P.T.A. once sponsored a hobby show at one of the schools, and we were asked to show a frame of some of our very early Shrub Oak letters. It excited considerable interest. Most of the so-called "first families" of Shrub Oak ("first" only in the sense that one is not a native of the town until he has seen his grandparents buried in the local cemetery) trace their lineage

12

back many generations. They boast of their Americanism, apparently unmindful of the fact that their ancestors were Tories throughout the Revolution, and that they gave scant aid or comfort to the colonial cause. Far from ever having slept there, Washington regularly circumvented the town on his occasional journeys from Peekskill, some five miles away. Peekskill was Washington's headquarters during the Revolution for a longer period of time than any other place.

The collection's popularity lay in the fact that the names on each envelope were the same names that appear on mailboxes along the highway. They were in the society columns of the local papers, and on the committees which are appointed to further important civic causes, such as the height above the ground at which the lower limbs of trees are to be kept, or the fight against street lights, lest the young of the town be encouraged to congregate under them at night.

On this particular occasion the frame of Shrub Oak covers was given a place of honor on the wall, where it could readily be seen just alongside a beautiful exhibit of hand crocheting. Both exhibits received considerable attention from the spectators. On the second day of the show, when we decided to visit it, we were pleased that a line—not a large one, but nevertheless definitely a queue—had formed before the two exhibits. A twelve-year-old boy was stationed nearby to answer inquires. The lady just ahead of us asked, "Is the crochet exhibit for sale?" The youth replied negatively. "No, the crocheting is not for sale, but the old letters are. They're $5.00 for everything."

The questioner expressed regret that the crocheting was not for sale, and passed on to other exhibits. We asked the boy where he had obtained the information. He said that the previous day the lady in charge had told him that one frame was not for sale under any circumstances, while the other was priced at $5.00. We asked him if he was sure which was the one for sale, and, thinking, he admitted he may perhaps have confused the two frames.

We momentarily shuddered at the thought of seeing our local collecting activities of more than ten years change hands for the sum of $5.00, even aside from the fact that the frame had cost us considerably more. But it showed us quite emphatically that value is value only when it is recognized as such, and that without demand value might as well be nonexistent.

This is what we find one of the most difficult points in philately to get across.

One of the earliest cross-country flights by air was one sponsored by a soft-drink concern. The ancient plane took many, many days to make the journey in the course of which it spent more hours on the ground than in the air. Covers carried on the flight are known even today as "Vin Fiz" covers, and they fetch a price well into the hundreds of dollars. They are rare, but, more to the point, they are popular.

On a recent anniversary of the flight some persons decided to re-enact the flight with a plane of somewhat more modern aspect but following the same route. To finance it, the plane was loaded with approximately five hundred covers, which would be sold to a breathlessly awaiting public on the flight's completion.

We (and perhaps a number of other auctioneers as well) were offered the rare opportunity to place one of these 500 covers in one of our auction sales, subject only to certain conditions under which it was to be sold. The most important condition was, of course, the price at which it was to be sold, for something as rare as this could not be permitted to sell for a price anywhere near its actual value (which at least in our opinion was nil). We declined the opportunity to handle it, perhaps not so graciously as we should have in the eyes of the owners.

For without demand the factor of supply is of little consequence. The old adage about selling refrigerators to Eskimos is well taken. It is not that a refrigerator is not a useful, perhaps even a necessary device, but the market for it is greater along the Equator than it is above the Arctic Circle. And if there are no patrons with sufficient funds along the Equator to buy it, its value there is little different than it would be five thousand miles farther north.

Stamp magazines today are full of columns written by tipsters purporting to predict which stamps are on the way "up." Dealers fill up their ads with such statements as "only 100,000 issued," or "only 25,000 available for distribution in the United States," or "printed in smaller numbers than the twenty-four-cent air-mail invert." Unfortunately many buyers are taken in by the comparison, which is invidious at best.

Collectors sometimes find it difficult to understand why, for example, the $5.00 stamp of 1902 (Scott #313) catalogues at $145, while the very same stamp, surcharged for use in the Philippine Islands, of which only a fraction as many were issued, lists at only $85. Another stamp, the three-cent United States stamp of 1923–26 perforation ten, lists at $3.50; in 1927 it was surcharged for use in the Canal Zone. The latter stamp was issued perhaps in one tenth, maybe even one twentieth the quantity of the former, but it now catalogues at only sixty cents. The reasons are not difficult to fathom; there are far more collectors seeking the much more common unsurcharged stamp in each case than those who seek the other. It is a basic fact that the collecting of United States stamps is infinitely more popular than the collecting of stamps of the United States possessions.

But one need not compare the stamps of one issuing entity with corresponding stamps of another. It is doubtful whether anyone knows how many of the fifty-cent postage-due stamp (Scott #J 58) were issued in perforation ten. The Bureau of Engraving and Printing simply did not think it important to keep records of such comparative trivialities as perforation differences, whatever the significance in which they are held by philatelists. Judging by its scarcity, our feeling is that only a few thousand of them were issued. Not one in a thousand dealers has it in stock; one seldom sees it offered in an auction catalogue. Certainly a rare stamp such as the $4.00 Columbus (Scott #245) is far more frequently available; there is hardly an auction catalogue listing United States stamps that does not offer at least one specimen. Despite this incongruity, the more common four-dollar Columbus brings from four to eight times the price of the far rarer postage-due.

The Scott catalogue lists a number of stamps of which but a few dozen at best exist; one of these, a specimen surcharge on a one-cent executive stamp issued on soft porous paper, catalogues at $1.75. In some thirty years we have seen exactly three copies. Yet the aforementioned twenty-four-cent air-mail stamp of 1918, with the inverted center, of which one entire sheet of one hundred were issued, and of which the majority are still on the market on various occasions, last sold for almost ten thousand dollars!

No one can possibly question the statement, therefore, that supply is a factor only in relation to demand. The collection of early Shrub Oak covers was of considerable value to ourselves; undoubtedly any stamp dealer who might have been present at the P.T.A. exhibition would have grabbed it for $5.00, and perhaps ten times that price, but in the market in which it was offered for sale, over a period of two days, no one considered it was worth five dollars, and for that we remain most thankful.

During the Roosevelt administration Guatemala issued a souvenir sheet, one of the four figures on it being President Roosevelt. It wasn't particularly popular, and although Guatemala collectors felt obliged to include it in their collections, not too many others did. But in 1945, when F.D.R. died, its existence was suddenly recalled, and as nations all over the world issued stamps commemorating the wartime president, the demand for it was greatly stimulated. It was so in demand that the price zoomed from a nominal figure to $3.25. The number in existence had not varied; the supply was fixed; only the demand for it had increased. Collectors were happy to pay full catalogue, and, in some cases, more for an example of it. Then, when the Roosevelt fever died, as the fever does sooner or later with all such topical issues, demand for it died down. Today, while it catalogues at the same price, it can be sold only if the discount from catalogue price is sufficiently large to tempt a buyer who finds that he can continue his philatelic career equally well with it or without it.

Similarly, when in 1933 the then British Colony of Newfoundland decided to picture various members of the royal family on its stamps, one of those shown was a royal infant named Princess Elizabeth. No one could possibly foresee then that this child, far down in the line of succession for the throne, might someday be the queen. The stamp was not overly popular, but with the abdication of King Edward VIII and the accession of King George VI, the line of succession changed. Overnight the realization that someday the infant shown on this Newfoundland stamp (Scott #192) would be Queen of England created such a demand for the stamp that its catalogue value increased to $5.00.

There are not infrequent occasions when, despite an increase in the supply of an item, the demand for it will so increase that paradoxically, its increased availability will make for an increased price.

When in 1917 the Bureau of Engraving and Printing chose to use a new perforation dimension on its stamps it of course created a new philatelic variety. For three years before 1917 it had been issuing its stamps with what is known as perforation ten. When difficulties in tearing the stamps apart with this perforation became evident, it was decided to place the perforations a trifle closer together, thus resulting in the issue known as "perforation eleven."

In arranging the plate of the two-cent stamps, an act of carelessness resulted in the inclusion of three five-cent stamps in what should have been a sheet of 400 two-cent stamps. The stamps were widely distributed over the country, and sold in thousands of post offices before many alert philatelists noticed the error. A notice went out from Washington that every sheet of two-cent stamps bearing the plate number 7942 was to be taken off sale and returned to Washington. By that time many thousands of them had been sold; it will never be known how many. When it was discovered that the "five-cent error," as it is called, also existed in sheets with perforation ten, it was readily seen that the careless error had occurred before the change over from perforation ten had been ordered.

So common were these errors that one stamp magazine, *Weekly Philatelic Gossip,* offered a block of two-cent stamps, one of them with the five-cent error, with every new subscription for the magazine at twenty-five cents. Today that same block in perforation ten lists at $150; in the more common perforation eleven, $90.00.

As was the custom at the time, a certain quantity of these stamps was issued imperforate in order to accommodate those large business houses that used automatic postage-affixing machines. The usual perforated stamps did not fit these machines; imperforate sheets, however, could be cut into rolls, and the machine could dampen, sever, and affix the stamp in one operation. An observant stamp dealer, suspecting that some of the imperforate sheets might also bear the telltale plate number 7942, called at the downtown New York post office on Park Row, torn down in the late 1930s. He was not disappointed. He

18

admitted having purchased about fifty sheets. It could not have been many more.

Each large sheet of 400 stamps (which were cut into more familiar panes of 100 stamps during the perforation operation) contained no less than three five-cent errors. In one pane of 100 there was but a single example; in another pane, there were two, one above the other. The remaining two panes of 100 each contained no five-cent stamps.

The fortunate finder offered the imperforate five-cent errors for sale at a price befitting their scarcity, but sales were none too brisk. News of the variety reached the ears of the eccentric millionaire Colonel E. H. Green, who in that period was literally spending a fortune for stamps. He arranged to buy the entire remaining supply, numbering approximately forty sheets.

After years of litigation the philatelic estate of Colonel Green was sold at auction in the 1940s. Collectors who had paid relatively large sums of money over the years for imperforate five-cent errors had reason to believe that their investment was ill-timed, for now a supply perhaps a hundred times what had previously been available was about to be thrown on the market.

The first sheet sold at auction brought a surprisingly high price, in excess of two thousand dollars. The price was right in line with the figure that blocks of the five-cent imperforate error had been bringing. Customary market value was about one thousand dollars per block; each imperforate sheet, although it contained three errors, as stated, consisted of two blocks of the error, one of them with the pair of stamps.

"Too high," said the smart boys. "Let's wait. There are forty-two yet to be sold, and the price will surely drop."

What was not realized was that the very fact that, now the error was more freely available than it had been, there was a greater demand for it than had previously existed. Many collectors would have liked to have purchased it before the Green

19

lot had come on the market, but seldom did they have the opportunity. Now, with prospects of there being more stamps available, a much greater number of buyers made their existence known. The next sheet sold brought an even higher price; successive sheets sold for even more.

Again demand had proven a greater and more potent factor than supply.

In 1940 the largest collection ever formed of the ninety-cent 1869, Scott #122, was offered at auction at a convention of the American Philatelic Society in Buffalo. It included almost four hundred examples of a stamp that was then so valuable that it regularly brought $50.00 per stamp when in presentable condition. Bidders at the sale "laid off" the first few dozen lots satisfied that when they were sold, the prices on the copies to be subsequently offered would drop to more reasonable levels. It turned out that the bargains were at the beginning of the sale, not at the end. Hundreds of collectors who did not have the ninety-cent 1869 decided to take advantage of their opportunity to obtain one, now that it was available. After the sale Scott found it necessary to increase the value of the stamp, not to decrease it. Today, two decades later, the effect of scattering such a large holding into hundreds of different collections has justified the present price of $135 for this stamp.

The history of the White Plains souvenir sheet, Scott #630, is another similar story. Only 107,398 of these little sheets of twenty-five stamps were issued to commemorate the International Philatelic Exhibition of 1926. With a face value of only fifty cents, all were sold out in a short time, at the Exhibition itself, and at the Philatelic Agency in Washington. It was not on sale at post offices other than the one in White Plains, New York, where a limited number were put on sale for first-day use.

So common was this for about five years that many holders decided to use them for postage. Since except for the size and the marginal descriptions it was precisely the same stamp as Scott #629 of which 40,639,485 were issued, single stamps, and even blocks, could not be told when used, once the marginal inscription was removed.

The second souvenir sheet was issued in 1933, partly to commemorate the Chicago World Fair of that year and partly to honor the American Philatelic Society's convention in that city in August. Issuance of this sheet caused many collectors to seek the earlier sheet of 1926, and a brisk boom in it started. By 1935 it had quadrupled in price, and it sold for $2.00. Fifteen years later it was bringing $7.50. Twenty years later it reached $10.00.

In the late 1950s the passing of a Washington, D.C., collector, Edward Meehan, disclosed that he had purchased a large part of the issue, reportedly twenty thousand sheets. In the intervening quarter century he had offered the sheets for sale to dealers as his financial needs dictated, always being careful that no more were offered than could be easily absorbed. With a rising market working in his favor, this was not difficult. At his death no more than a few hundred sheets remained in his estate, but knowledge of even this relatively small amount should have unsettled the market.

To the contrary, their sudden availability induced many collectors to seek examples whereas before this time they had been indifferent to them. The sheet had been bringing $32.50 prior to the liquidating of his philatelic estate; within a year the retail price reached $47.50, and it is still steadily rising.

It would be foolish to conclude from all this that the sudden availability of a large supply of even a popular stamp would result in substantial price increases. Without the concomitant of greatly increased demand, the laws of economics (which even philatelists cannot repeal) will result in a drop in price.

The boom in the stamps of Israel is an example of this.

There is a great appeal in the stamps of a new issuing entity.

21

Many collectors, realizing that they can never afford the earlier stamps of a given nation, try to get in "on the ground floor," as it were, by buying the first issue of a new country and continuing with each subsequent issue as it appears.

The dramatic effect of a nation such as Israel, reaffirming its sovereign existence after two thousand years, attracted thousands of collectors. Many purchased the stamps with little thought of future appreciation, simply to give needed funds to the tiny nation fighting for its life. Others no doubt purchased them with the thought that its days were numbered and that the 45,000,000 Arabs whose avowed determination to push the 800,000 Israelis into the sea would be successful, thus assuring that the stamps would be good property to own.

Israel's victory over the Arabs surprised a great many people, and more collectors rushed to collect these stamps, which were beautiful to behold, and which held such fine promise of appreciation. It became apparent that the limited numbers issued of the first series were scarcely sufficient to go around. Many another nation would have taken advantage of the situation by issuing more stamps for the revenue that might be obtained. Israel steadfastly refused. In a short time the first set of Israel, Scott #1-9, went from $8.50 per set to the fantastic figure of $250 per set.

The temptation to take a profit such as that was difficult for even Israel's stanchest supporters to resist. The purchases at intervening prices had not been made by the mass of collectors, but by a relatively small number of speculators who by their very actions removed from the market all available stamps as they were offered. The law of supply and demand was in full operation, and the price continued to increase. However, once those who had been buyers decided to take their profits and become sellers, a mild panic set in. When they could not get $250 per set, they dropped their price to $200, in order to protect their paper profits. They were surprised to find that there was no persistent demand even at $200, and disillusioned sellers offered the stamps for sale at $175, at $150, and finally at $125. With the supply increasing, and demand decreasing, prices reacted in accordance with the laws of economics.

The first set of Israel today brings around the one-hundred-dollar mark. This is a fine profit for those who bought it as a new issue at $8.50. It is a sad story for those who got in at the top. What the future holds for the set is a difficult thing to guess. There seems to be no great demand for it today. Collectors are no longer hysterical in their efforts to obtain one; most will buy it if advantageously offered. If it is not, they are content to wait.

Back in 1895 our Post Office issued a set of postage stamps with the highest value being a $100 stamp. The stamps were issued to pay the postage on newspapers, which, when sent in huge bulk, required so much postage that ordinary stamps would not suffice. Proud, indeed, was the collector who had the complete set in his collection, for it required an investment of $187.92—no insignificant sum for those days, and a respectable sum even today.

On July 1, 1898, use of the stamps was discontinued, and a more efficient method of collecting postage was adopted, one that is still in use today. Fortunate possessors of the sets were happy, and those who had neglected to obtain them regretted their imprudence. Philatelists in the stamp-magazine columns debated long and loud as to what disposition should be made of the unsold stamps, with those who had bought them for $187.93 insisting on their destruction and those who had not, seeking their availability at a nominal price.

It is to the shame of the Post Office Department that the motivating factor was not what would be best for philately, but which decision would bring in more money. In 1899 the Post

Office announced that the remaining stock would be sold at $5.00 per set to all who wished them. Seldom in philately does opportunity knock twice as it did then, and seldom when a nation with the philatelic responsibility of this one performs such an act.

The Post Office picked up $134,945 by its action, selling 26,989 sets with an original face value of $5,072,042. Business was so good that when the Department had more orders for sets than it had stamps on hand, it obligingly reprinted large quantities of the denominations from $5.00 to $100. Only the ultimate deaths of the numerous original buyers of these sets has stilled the clamor of protests which the sale engendered.

The disgust which the reprinting brought on lingers with us even today. While many of the earlier newspaper stamps today are extremely rare, with some cataloguing in the hundreds of dollars, the 1895 set now frequently brings less than the nominal $5.00 per set at which the Post Office sold them in 1899.

We thus encounter a new factor that has its part in affecting supply and demand: respectability. The increased supply of the 1895 newspaper stamps was, of course, sufficient to bring the price down, but the breaking of the faith that collectors had in the United States Post Office resulted in a disdain for the issue that remains to this day, despite the fact that not one in a hundred collectors is aware of the sordid story.

Happily the United States learned its lesson, with perhaps the only exception being the Farley scandal of 1935. Here, the issues were somewhat different, when stamps were reissued in order to make available to collectors certain stamps that had been surreptitiously issued and distributed to certain influential persons.

When in 1946 the Motor Vehicle Revenue stamps were discontinued, a clamor went up from philatelists to place them on sale for a nominal sum, so that those who had been reluctant to part with $136.43 (their original face value) might obtain them for less. Happily, the government refused.

There was a tremendous rush in 1935 to buy the Farley issue when they were put on sale in March of that year. Never before had the Philatelic Agency in Washington sold more than three million dollars' worth of stamps in a single year. Postmaster General Farley had indeed turned an error of judgment into a profitable deal for the Post Office. On some of the Farleys pitifully small quantities were issued. For example, on the souvenir pane of the three-cent Chicago, Scott #767, only 9,546 were issued, making it the smallest quantity known of any commemorative issue. Most collectors ignore it, however, since it too closely resembles the original three-cent Chicago pane, Scott #731, of which 441,172 were printed. Yet the former, despite its small quantity, lists at $8.50; the one that is by far more common, having been issued in almost fifty times the quantity, lists for $5.00!

Yes, demand is a more important factor than supply.

3. *Condition is a factor only in relation to value.*
There is a relatively small town in upper New York State called Camden. Aside from the fact that an approval house is located there, its philatelic renown today is minimal. But as an address it was well known a quarter century ago.

A lady collector of Camden set about gathering as many examples of the five-cent 1847, the first United States stamp, as she could after first setting a limit of $1.00 per stamp. Today such a pursuit would be ridiculous, for even the poorest copy of this stamp, if in half-decent presentable condition, would bring eight or ten times that figure.

Things were different in the mid 1930s, however. Our first stamp then had a catalogue value of only $8.50; exceptionally fine copies even then brought over catalogue, sometimes as high as double catalogue. The ordinary example brought $4.00 or $5.00, good-looking copies, in average condition. Those with defects generally had few buyers. When a fine copy of a stamp can be bought at a nominal price there is little demand for what are euphemistically called "space fillers." As we shall see later on, the rarer and more valuable a stamp is the greater the demand for it in defective condition.

The Camden lady, whose name unfortunately now escapes us, but whose treasure trove in all likelihood lies forgotten in some Camden attic, purchased many hundred five-cent 1847s

26

within her stated limit of $1.00 per stamp. She was a most useful outlet for the writer, and for several other dozen dealers to whom she had written, making her offer. Her checks were prompt, and never did she return a stamp or complain about the condition. Her invariable comment with each check was "Send more."

As things happen, she was soon priced out of the market by the market itself. It was no longer practical to sell even poor specimens for $1.00 each as the catalogue steadily increased. Our lady was not inclined to raise her limit, and by the mid-1940s, when the price of the stamp went up by leaps and bounds (in anticipation of its hundredth anniversary), her name was added to the inactive lists of all her previous suppliers.

Nothing has been heard from the lady from that day to this. Whether she is alive or not is a matter of conjecture; the present location of the stamps, or even whether they are still intact, can only be surmised.

But the point of the entire story is that we have here the case of a person buying only stamps in the poorest possible condition, who today, if she were alive, and in a position to do so, could obtain for them from five to ten times their original cost.

The moral is not that stamps in perfect condition are a splendid investment, nor that stamps in poor condition are a bad investment (the word "investment" being used in the philatelic sense), but that either or both can prove a very wise purchase if bought for what they are, at a price based on their actual condition.

We often read that stamps in absolutely perfect condition are gilt-edge investments. By and large this may be true, but we can cite offhand the experience of many collectors who were so taken with the magnificent condition of a certain stamp that they paid a price beyond all reason for it. We cannot gainsay their pride of possession, or their pleasure at showing it to all who will watch, but unless they are fortunate enough to find someone as eager as they were to buy it at the price which they had paid, the superb stamp can prove a poor investment.

No better off is the man who overpays on a defective stamp. He may be assured that the tiny thin spot or the slightly missing perforation is of little consequence, and without regard for the fact that whether minor or major, a defect is a defect, he buys the stamp at a price for which he should have obtained an undamaged one.

There is an album space waiting for every stamp in every conceivable condition, at a price.

Jack Spier of Spier Brothers, a firm of Montreal stamp dealers, once said to us: "I wasn't long in business when I stopped to think that about three-fourths of all the collections that I bought contained stamps in only average condition. It struck me that most collectors therefore were buying stamps in average condition, so why should I refuse this business? I'll buy any stamp today, always at a price in keeping with its condition, and I find that any stamp sells—at a price in keeping with its condition."

It's fine to preach the gospel of perfection. We have many times advised our own friends to collect the best. If it is worth collecting at all, it is worth buying only in the finest possible condition. This is good advice for the most part ... if one can afford to take such advice. But only a very small portion of the body philatelic is in a position to take it.

One might as well advise the American public to eat only filet mignon and to refuse to buy chuck steak; to buy only de-luxe cars, and to decline the purchase of the less expensive, more economical cars; to travel only first-class on planes.

This would wreak havoc with the meat packers, for only a tiny portion of each beef produces the filet mignon; the automobile manufacturers, each putting out only one model—the best, would find their market limited; and the plane companies would soon find that they had lost the bulk of their passengers.

The fact is that while no one can question that it is always best to buy the finest quality, the cold reality is that not everyone can afford it. This is no less true in stamps.

We have leafed through stamp albums on frequent occasions, with the owner showing the way. This is a task that every stamp dealer must undergo with some degree of regularity. He has perhaps seen nothing but stamps all day long in his office, but that evening his client or even his house guest must trot out the album and turn page by page, explaining to the dealer the most elementary remarks about every stamp and every set. But common courtesy usually demands that he be a respectful listener. (However, when the collection being shown consists of the monotonous repetition of similarly decorated first-day covers, or even worse, matched-plate block sets, it is difficult to be both respectful and a listener.)

During these leafing excursions we have found that the pleasure a collector gets from his collection bears no relation whatsoever to what he has paid for the stamps or the condition in which they are. We have been bored stiff looking at a collection of immaculate, perfectly centered stamps, with the owner reciting his cost on each and every one. We have been entranced with a recital of another collector, showing stamps which another might suggest be consigned to the ashcan, but which come to life as each postmark, the characteristics of each issue, are explained.

As Mr. Spier remarked, someone buys these stamps.

A man of principle is always to be admired. A man who sets high standards, and refuses to compromise them always earns the admiration of the world. We have met many in philately who have earned this accolade. We know better than to show them a stamp which deviates the slightest extent from perfection. We do not suggest that they do not know what they are doing, nor even that their collection does not bring them the same amount of satisfaction that another might. It just does not necessarily follow that it does.

"Buy only the best and you will not regret it," the advice is given. But it is not always the best advice.

In our Nassau Street days, when the Kansas–Nebraska issue of 1929 was still available at perhaps one-sixth of today's price, a collector visited our offices. The trade has a name for people of his kind; it is used without malice, and most collectors would hardly take umbrage at the designation: condition crank. Some, in fact, are proud of it. No dealer ever objected to doing business with a condition crank as long as the crank knows that stamps in perfect condition are seldom found, and, when available, sell at prices considerably above those of the ordinary run.

They do sometimes lose patience with an individual such as one who once entered our offices seeking a stamp "for a gift to a little boy." It could be just any old stamp, as long as it was in perfect condition, but the main requirement was that it must be cheap, "since it was a gift." That particular individual spent more in shoe leather up and down Nassau Street than he did in dollars, always looking for perfect stamps "for the little boy"— but they must be "cheap."

Such individuals of course are occasionally accommodated, as we shall see later.

To return to the Kansas-Nebraska customer: on many occasions we showed him sets of blocks of these stamps which, while in exceptionally fine condition, were somewhat below the standard that he had set. When two years passed without his having the set, and the price steadily increasing, we made two suggestions to him. One was that he buy a really fine set when it presented itself and continue the search for the set he had thus far been unable to find.

"Then when you find it," we suggested, "you can sell the set you then have. If the market has improved, you will be able to get for the first set you purchased a price increased to the same degree that the market has increased."

This he declined to do. We made a second suggestion.

"It may cost you more to buy them individually, but at least you will be buying at the going market in each instance, and ultimately you will have the complete set in the condition in which you wish them."

This he also declined to do. It had to be the complete set, and it had to be absolutely perfect. The price was not an issue.

Of course he ultimately did obtain the set. As it so happened, by today's standards he obtained a bargain, although at the time of purchase it was probably the highest price ever paid for a set of Kansas–Nebraska blocks. But had he bought one of the exceptionally fine sets that had been offered him years earlier, and sold it when the set of his choice came along, the high price that he ultimately had to pay would have been reduced considerably.

There are any number of fetishes to which collectors succumb. The demand for original gum on the back of stamps is one of them. It is futile to suggest that gum should be done away with. Regularly well-meant suggestions are made that the presence or absence of gum be ignored. Some have suggested that the catalogue adopt another classification: unused with gum, unused without gum, and used. (A minor adaptation of this was actually done at one time when the Scott catalogue listed some early issues at two prices, with and without original gum. It failed to still the clamor.)

A dealer of a half century ago, Eustace Power, the then owner of Stanley Gibbons, Inc., made the remark so often heard: "The most valuable commodity in the world is not radium, it is gum, for collectors are paying at the rate of a million dollars per gallon for it." The statement, if anything, is conservative, for a bit

31

of gum that would scarcely tilt an apothecary's scale has, on frequent occasions, added a few hundred dollars to the value of a stamp.

The situation is one that some individuals turn to their advantage. We know one chap who engaged in a prodigious amount of philatelic research in Washington. It was so rewarding that he finally came up with the exact formula for the gum that was applied to the Columbus Exposition issue of 1893. The formula for Coca-Cola is a guarded one, and has perhaps brought its owners a veritable fortune, but not far behind it in remunerative possibilities is the formula for "government gum." There are no figures, nor will there ever be, for the number of so-called mint stamps which have actually been regummed. While perhaps 80 per cent or even 90 per cent of all regummed stamps can be told at a glance, there are many on which even the most informed experts will disagree. When one remembers that the official formula was changed from time to time, and that often on the same issue, two distinct types of gum are definitely known to have been used, the possibilities become apparent.

The advice is given to buy stamps only from reputable sources. This, too, is fine advice, but any reputable dealer will testify that he has seen stamps with gum on the back that he might hesitate to declare as original. Our most impartial and learned expert committees have sometimes found it necessary to reverse their own opinions on the subject.

We leave it to the better judgment of the collector whether the payment of a tremendous premium for a stamp is justified because the gum is immaculate on the back, and without the slightest sign of a hinge.

Given two stamps that are identical in condition, in appearance, in shade, and in every philatelic consideration except for the back, we would unhesitatingly state that the stamp that has been lightly hinged will be the better buy, assuming, of course, that the asking price for the unhinged specimen is in keeping with the present market tendencies.

The situation becomes absolutely absurd when it is applied to stamps of modern vintage. The myth that a hinged stamp might as well be damaged is widely believed by juvenile collectors as well as ignorant adult collectors. A perfect specimen that has been hinged will be refused with disdain at a dollar or two in favor of one that has never been hinged at double or triple the price. One can scarcely blame the dealer; the demand for the latter stamp and its inadequate supply force him to ask the higher price, for when he buys the stamp, he, too, is asked to pay more. The dealer when he buys can dictate neither the price nor the condition of the stamp he is about to buy. He must buy it or decline its purchase—unless he is one with access to original gum, for which he can charge the equivalent of a million dollars per gallon.

There are any number of wise collectors who foresee what we feel is an inevitable conclusion to the gum fetish. They are buying perfect stamps, but without gum, at correspondingly low prices. The wisdom of the effort is already to be seen. Even the auction catalogues today uniformly state that gum is not to be expected on stamps before 1890, unless its presence is expressly mentioned. The year 1890 is not an arbitrary date. It was chosen because the gum fetish had its beginnings with the Columbus Exposition issue of 1893, at which time the 1890 series was being sold concurrently at post offices. Before 1890 philately has a pitifully small backlog of mint stamps on which to draw.

The prejudice against hinges blossomed with the appearance of stamp mounts. The invention of cellophane in the 1920s led to its use by many collectors who were seeking to protect their stamps. Within a few years most of these found, to their chagrin, that cellophane, far from protecting their stamps, would actually damage them because of the obnoxious materials that went into its manufacture, obnoxious as far as the stamps themselves were concerned.

The invention of cellulose acetate for stamp mounts was a step in the right direction, and, when properly used, and when properly manufactured, one may feel relatively secure that his stamps will be adequately protected, unless he happens to live in a humid climate. (It must be mentioned that under those circumstances the use of hinges is equally ill-advised.)

The irony of the situation is that the widest use of acetate mounts is among the collectors of modern, easily-obtained stamps, the very ones on which gum in pristine condition adds nothing at all to the value of the stamp. We can state without fear of contradiction that not one of the many magnificent valuable collections of classics in the world, amassed by some of the most informed collectors who ever lived, is kept in acetate mounts.

The pinnacle of philatelic acceptability is an invitation to exhibit in one of the international exhibitions, at which usually only the cream of philately is on view. Rules for exhibiting may vary from country to country, but invariably one condition expressed is that stamps cannot be exhibited when in acetate mounts. An advanced collector, one who certainly knows his way in philately, does not hesitate to mount his choicest acquisition with a good hinge.

Even more in the realm of absurdity is the ignorant collector who insists that all his stamps be unhinged at the time of purchase, but who recognizes the desirability of hinges by then hinging the stamp into his album. The height of folly was a collection we once were proudly shown by a collector; under each stamp he had professionally written: "Unhinged before being hinged." That description would apply to every stamp ever manufactured.

As with everything else, there are exceptions. Were one to obtain a stamp that is actually unique, without ever having been touched by a hinge, the owner would be justified in hesitating to apply a hinge to the gummed surface. But such a decision is given to very few to make. But even the word "unique" is subject to its philatelic interpretation, for the word is often abused in our hobby. The late auctioneer Max Ohlman once described a certain stamp in his auction catalogue as "unique," and he then followed with three more lots, each described as "an identical lot." By definition, use of the word "unique" insists that no other can exist.

At what price is a stamp without gum a more desirable purchase than one with gum? Happily, there is a rule of thumb on this which one may profitably follow. That is to examine the price of the same stamp in *used* condition.

There seems little reason why a stamp without gum should sell for less than the same stamp in used condition, except for the very few instances where the stamp in legitimate used condition is extremely rare. One outstanding exception is the ninety-cent one of 1860, Scott #39. This stamp was distributed to post offices a few months before the outbreak of the War Between the States. Postmasters in the seceded states declined to surrender their stamp stocks to the Post Office in Washington; the Federal authorities countered by demonetizing the entire issue. Relatively few of the stamps were ever used, while quantities of them lay for years in southern offices, unsought, since they had no validity. Today the stamp is scarce even in unused condition, but with a postmark of undisputed legitimacy it is a real rarity. Even the commonest stamp in this set, the three-cent, lists at almost double the price in a used block that it does in an unused block. (This presents a wonderful opportunity to those who are willing to simulate the proper postmarks of a century ago with a modern reproduction. Happily, since today's ink is entirely different from that once used, these can ordinarily be told by an expert.)

Aside from these exceptions, an unused stamp without gum, which is available at less than the price of the same stamp used, is a mighty fine bargain that any collector should be quick to take advantage of. There are many stamps that sell for virtually the same price, used or unused. This is true of many of the relatively scarce commemoratives, such as the Norse-Americans, some of the 1901 Pan-Americans, and some of our early air mails. Many of the relatively common "two-cent reds" of the period between 1926 and 1932 are actually scarcer in used condition than in mint, if one judges by the quantities available on the market. A dealer can buy large quantities of these in mint condition with far greater ease than he can buy the same stamp in a similar quantity in used condition, even though the latter may catalogue a lesser amount. The answer, of course, is the unfortunate fact that ordinarily there is a greater demand for the mint.

The mass approval houses are able to take advantage of this situation. For every collector who visits a stamp store and asks his dealer to show him a two-cent Von Steuben, Scott #689, for example, there are perhaps a dozen collectors in some part of the country, without access to a stamp shop, who will buy that same stamp from an approval sheet. Many dealers find it profitable to buy quantities of these stamps mint and to affix them to their return envelopes. When they send the approvals out, the stamped envelope accompanies for their return. Collectors, as a general rule, appreciate such a generous and thoughtful act as prepaying the return postage, although it must be admitted that there are approval recipients who will toss a monkey wrench into the proceedings by appropriating the stamp and replacing it with a current, and a common, one.

Nevertheless, a dealer can build up a stock of these much

scarcer used stamps at very moderate cost while at the same time offering this gesture of generosity to his client. When one recalls that in used condition the very real prejudice against badly centered stamps does not exist to the same degree that it does with mint stamps, the added margin of incentive becomes even more apparent. The collector of used stamps in addition does not trouble his dealer with the annoying custom of demanding a stamp untouched by a hinge.

Collecting customs are changing today. Not long ago even knowledgeable collectors looked with disfavor upon a stamp with a defect, no matter how otherwise exceptional it might be. An old-time collector, Ernest Jacobs of Chicago, whose judgment on the condition of our early stamps was not to be disputed by anyone, once spotted a twenty-four-cent purple of 1870–71 (Scott #153) in our stock. It was of truly exceptional appearance in every way, but we felt obliged to apologize for the fact that it had a minor defect. Jacobs had an exceptional memory with regard to stamps; he recalled the circumstances of purchase of almost every stamp in his collection. Each time we met he reminded us that one of his finest purchases was that particular stamp. When his collection was sold shortly after his death, the bidding on that particular stamp was heated. It brought three times the catalogue price despite the defect!

Condition in stamps is a factor only in relation to value.

4. *There is no substitute for knowledge.* There is no other hobby engaged in today that possesses the vast amount of literature that philately can boast of, even though, considering the millions of collectors there are reputed to be, our philatelic books are published in quantities of a few thousand.

The largest of our stamp publications, *Linn's Weekly Stamp News,* has a circulation of less than seventy-five thousand. This is more than double the circulation of the next largest magazine. The aggregate circulation of all stamp weeklies, even without allowing for the inevitable fact that many collectors take two or even three or four magazines, is less than two-hundred thousand.

Our largest stamp society, the American Philatelic Society, which, incidentally, is the largest assemblage of stamp collectors in the world, numbers less than fifteen thousand members. The Society of Philatelic Americans, in second place, has half that number. The aggregate membership of all our national stamp societies, again ignoring the inevitable duplication (most advanced collectors belong to *all* of them), runs to perhaps 35,000.

The leading stamp catalogue, published by Scott Publications, declines to give any figures as to how many it issues annually, but the trade generally assumes it is about seventy-five thousand.

The competitive catalogue, issued by Minkus Publications, like-wise declines to state the number printed, but it is doubtful whether it exceeds that number.

Where do the countless. hundreds of thousands of hidden collectors obtain their information? The only answer that one can come up with is that they do not seek any.

Some may question that there are that many collectors. While such figures as 20,000,000 are fanciful (James A. Farley, when postmaster general, gave that figure as his estimate), there can be no doubt that the number must exceed a million, and there is reason to believe that it runs much higher.

An associate, Colin McNaught of Wellington, New Zealand, once shipped us a quarter million copies of one of the cheapest and most common stamps in the catalogue, the one-penny New Zealand stamp showing their native bird, the kiwi. He then offered the holding to a dozen American dealers, instructing each that in the event that he could use it the lot was in the United States and that prompt shipment could be made. It was more efficient to handle it in this way than to have the stamps in New Zealand, from which it might take three months to ar-range delivery. A quarter of a million of anything is a prodi-gious quantity; even in a tiny commodity such as stamps it makes a large parcel.

The stamps were subsequently ordered by an approval firm in upstate New York, Jamestown Stamp Company, and the stamps were shipped, and we proceeded to forget the trans-action. Less than two years later an inquiry came from James-town, New York: could we offer them more one-penny kiwis? We could not, nor could Mr. McNaught amass a similar quan-tity, and we advised Jamestown to that effect. At the same time we could not resist asking what they had done with a quarter million examples of the same stamp. The reply was not long in coming, but even before it came we knew the answer. They had sold them.

It seems incredible that in the course of a little more than a year a quarter of a million collectors, most of them undoubtedly juveniles, had received an approval selection, and, being attracted to that particular very common stamp, had removed it, and remitted for it the price of one penny. (We assume, of course, that this one stamp was not the total amount of their purchase; were it so, the Jamestown company would not be the important firm that it is.)

One might easily regard it as of little consequence that these 250,000 buyers of stamps cared little about increasing their philatelic knowledge. Unfortunately, too many of our supposedy intelligent adult collectors are as uninterested.

Not long ago we were called to an exclusive residential neighborhood on Long Island to look at a collection which was for sale at a price of $15,000. The owner was a very successful individual in the carpeting business with a name known to many readers of the New York press because of his large advertisements. He had branches in all five boroughs of New York City; his home bespoke his wealth and apparently his keen business acumen, which had resulted in such outstanding success in his field.

The collection was disappointing; it was not even a collection. Mr. Tabrizzian (which was not his name) had made an arrangement with a number of postal clerks to save for him the corner plate number blocks from sheets of commemoratives. Although contrary to postal regulations, such acts are by no means unusual. Many post-office employees supplement their modest earnings by removing the plate number blocks from the sheets in their drawers and holding them for a friend who rewards them for their loyalty. Although the Post Office inspectors are ever on the alert for such actions, it is a very difficult thing to determine. (Although not an illegal act in itself, Uncle Sam has never looked with favor on anyone profiting from a deed from which he cannot demand a share of the proceeds.)

Mr. Tabrizzian's holdings had a face value of more than ten thousand dollars. He had arrived at his asking price of $15,000 by a simple device. Each block was in a glassine envelope; there were almost 100,000 envelopes which had cost him almost $500. His rewards to the various post-office clerks ran to another $500, making a total cost of $11,000, and for his trouble, and profit on his "investment," assigning to stamps perhaps the markup he assigned to selling carpets, $15,000 seemed like a fair price.

It wasn't, nor were we interested in purchasing the lot. To the beginner the collecting of modern commemorative plate number blocks may be the most desirable thing to do, but in practice the amassing of such items in tremendous quantities is about the poorest investment in the philatelic field. The ease with which one can be obtained at the post office at face value makes the sale of several hundred of a single variety, if not impossible, then at least difficult. And since even those who for one reason or another miss the opportunity to purchase one at face value at the post office, can buy it for a few cents additional from a dealer, the notion that the world is waiting to buy the senseless accumulation is a mistaken one.

We were interested in what had prompted Mr. Tabrizzian into such a dilemma. We received the age-old reply: how could he possibly do other than make money, since they were always worth face value? The faulty premise needs no correction here; we can only assume that every reader of this book is well aware of the foolishness of such a statement.

But there was one thing we had noticed that made us wonder. All of Mr. Tabrizzian's plate number blocks were in blocks of six, although most of them were stamps printed by the rotary

41

press which even neophyte philatelists know are collected in blocks of four. Mr. Tabrizzian supplied the answer.

"I never was able to understand why some commemoratives were collected in blocks of four and some in blocks of six, so to make sure that I did it right, I collected them all in blocks of six."

This seemed a startling admission for a smart businessman to make, a man, incidentally, willing to "invest" $10,000 in a hobby. We asked him if he knew the difference between a rotary-press stamp, which is of course collected in a plate number block of four, and a flat plate stamp collected in a block of six. He recalled having heard the words.

"I never could tell which was which," he replied.

We left Mr. Tabrizzian with his plate blocks, wondering, at the same time, how anyone could be so foolish as to spend a sum of money like that without knowing the most basic thing about the very items he was buying.

While Mr. Tabrizzian's is perhaps an extreme case, any dealer can testify that it is by no means unusual. Millions of dollars are being spent for stamps each year in this country by people who, were they buying a pair of shoes, a house, or an automobile, would first take the trouble to know at least a little about the object of their purchase.

How many collectors, when arranging their collections, do not trouble to check the perforations of each stamp? Worse yet, how many even know how to use a perforation gauge? We have purchased many collections with each stamp neatly hinged in place, with the hinge affixed upside down, so that far from fulfilling its destiny as a "hinge" to lift the stamp, it has been so affixed that if one attempts to lift the stamp, it neatly creases in the middle.

How many collectors know how to use the Scott catalogue? The first few pages of the Scott catalogue contain the finest exposition of stamp collecting, its vocabulary, its practices, and its customs that one can find anywhere. How many have read it? How many actually own a Scott catalogue? And even if the cost of the catalogue is beyond reach, how many have consulted one at a nearby public library? Most libraries possess one, even if it may not be the most recent edition.

It is a proud boast of philatelists that they are the most informed people in the world. Granted that they can be, with even a modest desire to learn something about their stamps, the fact is that by far the greater number are collecting in the dark. How else can one explain the relatively small circulation of stamp magazines, the small membership rolls of stamp societies, the small sale of stamp catalogues?

Yet knowledge of what one is doing, what one is buying, what one's collecting goals are, remains the most necessary thing in the world, especially when one is spending money for something which he hopes will someday pay him a profit.

One does not have to memorize the catalogue, as the saying goes, nor even to identify stamps on sight without reference to a catalogue, although such an ability is certain to offer important dividends. A familiarity with the catalogue, a knowledge of where to get desired information is invaluable. In short, there is no substitute for knowledge.

An important rule to follow is that any item listed in the Scott or the Minkus catalogue has an aura of respectability about it. This is not necessarily to say that anything not listed in the catalogue is to be left strictly alone; wisdom that comes from experience will tell when one should avoid like the plague and when one should welcome the opportunity to buy an item well beyond the pale. For, respected though our catalogues are, there still are items in them which would be better left out— and items that perhaps someday will receive the seal of approval.

There is little valid reason for including Christmas seals or even telegraph stamps in a catalogue of postage stamps. Neither could perform the function of a postage stamp. But they are listed, and quite competently, too, and on the basis of the listings one does have an idea of comparative values. But wisdom presumes a knowledge of the fact that Christmas seals issued after about 1916 are just so much waste paper. While this may be denied, it seems to be pretty factual that vast quantities of Christmas seals in sheets back more than forty years are still in existence, and that they can be bought by dealers at most advantageous prices. The nominal face value of one cent per stamp is meaningless; we know of Christmas seals from as long ago as thirty years for which the price of one cent *per sheet* was a difficult one to obtain.

Knowing this fact is not to deny that many of the rarer Christmas seals are rare, and worth their weight in uranium. This is a general rule applicable to any field of collecting which is not too popular. This applies to entire envelopes, to cut squares, to precancels, to revenues. The rule of thumb simply is that in those fields where the cheaper and medium-grade items are difficult to sell, the greater rarities sell extremely well.

Let us take cut squares, for example. A single stamp that catalogues up to $5.00 or so will generally be freely available at retail for about half catalogue. Grouped with others of similar value in an auction lot, it should bring from a fourth to a third of catalogue, or even less. But when a cut square comes along in the $50.00 or $100 class, full catalogue or more is most likely the rule. When it becomes a $1,000 item, to coin a phrase, the sky is the limit.

The reason is obvious: only the wealthier collector is in a position to seek the more expensive item. He already has the cheaper, and many of those who might need the less expensive are waiting their chance to pick it up advantageously. The man seeking a rarity knows better than to wait, for he may not have the opportunity soon again.

A knowledge of stamps that are known to exist, even though not listed in the catalogue, can pay off handsomely. Two well-known United States stamps come to mind. Although the blue-paper issue of 1909 is thoroughly listed, the Scott catalogue says nothing at all of a contemporary issue printed on paper that was mixed not with rag content (which produced Scott #357-366 and #369) but with a product called China clay. The paper difference is quite readily noticeable, and specialists include specimens in their collections. Although rarer than the more common blue-paper, the China clay does not bring so much, but knowledge of its existence will certainly enable the fortunate possessor, once the stamp has been proven to be the variety, to obtain a considerable premium for it over the more common regular variety.

For some reason Scott refuses to list a thirty-cent Franklin perf. 10 stamp without a watermark, although there seems to be little question that it exists. The Minkus catalogue appears convinced of its existence, as is everyone in the stamp field with the exception of Scott. It is known in a complete sheet, in blocks, in singles, and in used copies. Knowledge of this stamp's existence can easily offer profitable moments when they turn up among the more common stamp known as Scott #439.

The six-cent and the eight-cent of the 1895 issue, both very common stamps, were issed in error on revenue paper. Whereas the paper intended for the series was watermarked "U.S.P.S." for United States Postal Service, a quantity were printed on paper watermarked "U.S.I.R." (United States Internal Revenue). They can be found with no great difficulty if one knows what to look for; of course one must find the letters "I" or "R" unmistakably clear to prove the stamp; unfortunately, the letter "U" or "S" might come from either the normal or the error.

In used condition the six-cent lists at $100; in unused condition, $400. It has been our pleasant experience to have turned up examples of both on more than one occasion. Even the much more common eight-cent denomination lists at $200 and $17.50.

A knowledge of the manner in which collecting habits vary in different countries is a valuable asset. Our British cousins set a great store on inverted watermarks; in this country we are completely indifferent to them. Conceivably, all of our stamps could exist with watermarks inverted, but we have yet to find anyone remotely interested in their existence. Yet, even on some relatively common British stamps, such a variety would command a substantial figure.

The fact that we have a priceless volume such as the *Scott Specialized Catalogue* is a "built-in" guarantee of profitable buying if one has the good sense to use it.

The field of British revenue stamps is a fascinating one, but the unfortunate fact is that the Morley catalogue listing these issues is a half century old, and out of print. On the other hand, our Scott catalogue listings on revenues assures the comparatively ready market there is for them.

There are many collectors of such things as double perforations, double papers, paper folds, plate smears, and the like. Such things make interesting collections, and often they bring substantial prices. We only hope that those who buy some of these things at some of the almost fantastic prices asked for them realize that they are mere curiosities, simply freaks of printing and definitely not the errors they are often thought to be. On the other hand, a true error, such as an imperf between pair, a true double print, or a part perforate will always be sought by knowledgeable collectors, especially if blessed with a catalogue listing. A word of caution on part perforates would be in order; while a number of skipped or missing perfs between two stamps create an interesting item, they are not errors in the

philatelic understanding of the word. There must be no perforations for the entire length or width of a stamp for it to be
reckoned as a part perforate variety, and, equally important,
there can be no traces of perforations, commonly called blind
perfs.

There are two values of the 1917 issue, the two-cent and the
twenty-cent, which are often sold as part perforates but which
have barely noticeable traces of perforations. They do not break
the paper, and often they can be seen only with a strong glass,
but they are nevertheless occasionally offered by the ignorant,
and sometimes with full knowledge to the unsuspecting, as
Scott #499c (catalogue, $300) and #515b ($200). Their value
is negligible.

Often mere luck, coupled with a bit of knowledge, will permit one to get in on the ground floor of a field which later
achieves great popularity. Sometimes it is more than luck. Certainly those who faced the derision of the fraternity for twenty-
five years while collecting the bits of paper sent by rocket mail
have ample reason to be proud of themselves. Today hardly
anyone calls these "racket covers." We refused with disdain to
buy huge quantities of a label issued to carry a rocketful of mail
across the state line between New York and New Jersey in
1935. Today the two labels bring $20.00.

An approval dealer named George Wentz conceived a United
States-to-Mexico rocket flight across the Rio Grande where it
was probably no more than a trickle. For years he offered examples of this flown cover as approval premiums to encourage
collectors to buy his wares. Today they bring $20.00 or more. The
great advances in rocketry culminating with today's orbital
flights have given the field respectability, and now that they are
in demand, supplies seem nonexistent.

Other voices crying in the wilderness were raised in favor of
Arctic and Antarctic material. Some of this was unquestionably

of philatelic origin; much of it was absolutely authentic, being postmarks of early parties seeking either pole. Many letters from expeditions as long ago as the last century were available for prices not exceeding a dollar which today bring prices in the hundreds of dollars.

Many of those who put covers on some of our early airplane flights have seen their proud possessions bring a thousand times the original face value of the stamps and more. Unfortunately, many of these are not scarce, and it takes knowledge to tell the sheep from the goats. To confound matters even more, two of the outstanding pioneers in this field, who were responsible for many of these scarce items being available today, later cheapened their philatelic respectability by putting on the market similar covers, but with faked postmarks. Only an expert today can tell whether these pioneer air covers when addressed to A. C. Roessler of New Jersey are great rarities or rank counterfeits.

In the field of western covers, perhaps the most popular field of cover collecting today (as well as one in which covers bring the highest prices) there are names to beware of. The firm of Tandler and Company in San Francisco received a tremendous amount of correspondence in the early days of the West. Many of these legitimate covers with Wells Fargo postmarks fell into the hands of a stamp-dealer rogue from San Francisco, a Frenchman named Georges Carion. He attempted to add to their value by adding additional rare (but fake) postmarks to the legitimate ones already on the covers. Undoubtedly some Tandler covers with multiple postmarks are genuine; unfortunately, all are under a cloud unless passed by an expert. On the other hand, Tandler covers with but a single postmark are unquestionably genuine.

An entire book could be written on incidents of this sort. Few of the facts given here are found in books, yet they do appear regularly in our philatelic press. They are spoken of at stamp gatherings. Your favorite dealer will no doubt be willing to share others; advanced collectors, many of them with information on their pet fields far surpassing that of any dealer, are generally most willing to impart information. All that is needed is an audience.

The extent of the field of philatelic literature amazes anyone not familiar with it. While so-called "technical books" on collecting are not appearing today with the frequency they once did, because of increased publishing costs, the number being produced each year is still considerable.

Owing to the very nature of things, the number of books printed on any "technical" subject in stamps is limited. Often the publishing costs are not even returned to the publisher. Sometimes they are published at the expense of the author, simply in order to share his findings and his experience with collectors in general. (In few other fields does the researcher show such a willingness to share his discoveries not only without compensation, but often at considerable expense to himself.) Other times only by the unselfishness of a wealthy patron, such as the late Saul Newbury, of Chicago, does an angel appear to take over the costs of publishing a work.

The famed (and today, excessively rare) set of books on the one-cent stamp of 1851–57 by the late Stanley Ashbrook had most of its cost met by Mr. Newbury. Ashbrook offered a lifetime of study of this one stamp in the form of these books which were on sale for some years at $7.00 for the set. It is undoubtedly true that the illustrations in the books cost more than $7.00 per volume to produce.

Today the set of Ashbrook books has sold for as high as $70.00!

In 1934, following the sale of the George Walcott Collection of used Civil War patriotic covers, Robert Laurence of New

York was urged to produce the sale catalogue in bound form, with every one of the covers illustrated, and to append to it a list of the prices realized for each one. This was done; for fifteen years the greater part of the stockpile remained unsold. In an effort to get them into the hands of collectors, a deal was finally made whereby a publisher offered one as a free premium with each sale of a "book bundle" he was simultaneously advertising. Today the Walcott catalogue brings $20.00!

More recently, in 1947, H. L. Lindquist brought out the monumental *Nineteenth Century United States* by Lester Brookman. On sale for some years at the price of $10.00, the book eventually sold out, and only then did the demand for it ensue. Within a short time sets even in used condition were bringing $20.00; today sets have sold for as much as $30.00.

The ironic part of this mention of philatelic literature is that so much of it is available for so long a time at moderate prices and that, even if one completely disregards the vast fund of knowledge and information that is available to the reader, invariably at most moderate cost, the books are in almost every case a better investment than stamps themselves would be.

Our own earlier book, *Fancy Cancellations on Nineteenth Century United States Stamps,* was printed in a quantity of 3,250 copies, a rather large printing for a technical book. As a result, unsold quantities remained with us for eight years, despite our efforts to get it into the hands of readers, coupled with exhortations from other dealers with quantities to sell. When the last one was sold, an insistent demand ensued which continues so strong today that a single well-worn copy of it brought $16.00 at auction in New York in April 1962, as against the retail price of $5.00 at which it was available shortly before.

Collectors, no less than other solid citizens, are most liable to procrastination, and their sometimes naïve belief that because something is available today it will still be available tomorrow often causes them considerable financial loss. This is even more true in the case of philatelic literature. The small printings and the to-be-expected-continuing philatelic demand for a book on a popular subject (usually from collectors who show an interest in the subject in later years) cannot help but make purchase of the book a desirable investment, even if one chooses to be an ostrich philatelist, who refuses to read the book.

The authoritative book on Japan today brings $300; the one on Switzerland, $250. Both originally appeared at moderate prices. The Howes book on Canada, available for years at less than $10.00, has sold for $75.00, while the much more recently available Jarret book on the same subject was languishing on bookshelves for years at a $7.50 price (today it fetches $40.00).

Our remarks on the probabilities of price increase on philatelic literature unfortunately do not extend to such things as periodicals, annual catalogues, price lists, or "how-to" books. These are all indispensable, in the fullest sense of the word, but their appeal and their usefulness are limited in point of time. Only the so-called "dry" books, the technical ones, are the ones that are in steadily increasing demand as each year goes by.

But a philatelic education may be supplemented by other means than simply by reading books.

A liberal philatelic education can be obtained merely by studying the exhibits at a local, national, or international stamp exhibition. Yet how often at one of these shows does one find the crowd is at the bourse, buying stamps, while the exhibit hall itself is comparatively empty.

One should not concentrate on the so-called "blue-ribbon" collections at an exhibition. One may learn something from even the most modestly valued collections. Unfortunately, it is true that one may also pick up misinformation in such an instance, but the true seeker after knowledge should possess an inquiring mind and the ability to discard legend passed off as fact.

Even in the large international shows held every ten years there often is criticism of the judging. Judges being human, their personal prejudices can easily play a part in the awards. We have seen magnificent collections of a twentieth-century issue comparatively ignored because the judges were more favorably inclined to a collection of nineteenth-century classics. We once found a collection of precancels exceedingly interesting and well put together, to say nothing of their value, and one judge succeeded in prevailing over the others by insisting that precancels were of no interest.

We know that at one convention of a national philatelic society held in a western city within recent memory the judges were actually handed a list of names by the host committee, with instructions that these were to be the winners. Heading the list was an elderly collector whose days were numbered, and who had exhibited many times previously without winning an award. While the awarding of first prize to this gentleman was undoubtedly an act of extreme thoughtfulness, climaxing a lifetime of service to philately, it was hardly a graceful gesture to others who had entered the competition in good faith.

Perhaps one of the most unusual stories of philatelic judging was told us by that eminent husband-wife collecting team, Dr. and Mrs. Robert Breakey of Lansing, Michigan. They sought to include their exceptional prize-winning collection of the 1902 issue in an exhibition held by a national society in Chicago. The collection encompassed eight frames; it could not be shown in less, lest the factor of completeness, an important consideration in judging, be lost.

Although both Dr. and Mrs. Breakey had individual memberships in the society, they were told that no collection could occupy more than four frames and instructed to select just those pages which would not exceed four frames. Reluctant to break up the collection, they decided to exhibit as individuals, part of the collection under the name of Dr. Breakey, the balance as Mrs. Breakey's. Happily, they were at least united in the exhibit hall, so that the spectator could see the entire collection at one viewing. The judges, however, treated it as two collections; Mrs. Breakey won a first award; Dr. Breakey did not receive even an honorable mention.

But winning prizes, while engaged in by a great number of collectors, is certainly not the principal aim of most. To them, the pleasure of collecting, the thrill of the chase, the exhilaration that comes with final capture of the quarry, the wonderful experiences along the way remain the principal goal. And when one adds to these wonderful advantages the knowledge that he is buying wisely, and that perhaps when he tires of his collection his expenditure, far from having been in vain, will actually return him a profit, the sum total of philately's charm is visible.

But this pleasant aspect of collecting cannot be achieved by haphazard purchasing, by not taking advantage of the vast fund of knowledge available, or by ignoring certain rules that should be apparent to anyone who takes the trouble to think of them.

In short, there is no substitute for knowledge in philately.

5. *Don't be influenced by rumor or sentiment.*
When in early 1962, amid great secrecy, the Post Office prepared and distributed an issue of stamps to commemorate this country's first manned orbital flight, for some reason not stated the stamps that were issued the day of its accomplishment did not bear the legend "United States Postage." It created a stir among the noncollecting public.

Even *The New York Times,* which prides itself on its accuracy, often unjustifiably, added to the furor by stating that this was the first time that such an amazing omission had occurred. (It wasn't.) But many people who had never before thought of a postage stamp as other than a device to permit posting of a letter stampeded post offices to buy sheets of what the *Times* implied would be a great rarity. The Post Office, happy to capitalize on such a situation, obliged by issuing additional tens of millions of the stamps to meet the demand.

Decades from now disappointed "investors" will seek to "cash in their chips" and, finding that no one is interested, they will conclude that "investment" in stamps is a bad business. So it has been, for them.

Every philatelist during those weeks encountered some of these sheep, who thought they were "investing." Our reply to most of them left them somewhat bewildered: "Bring us one that *does* say on it 'United States Postage' and we'll give you

$10,000 for it; we wouldn't pay four cents for an example without it."

Regularly throughout philatelic history rumors and, less often, sentiment, have played their part in the stamp market. If only the ignorant and the uninformed were the victims of this state of affairs, it would not be so bad. Too often stamp collectors who should know better are carried away.

The coin field has its counterpart. Perhaps there has been no new coin issued in this century that has not been greeted with the baseless rumor that an error has been found on it, and that it has been "recalled." The word "recalled" is the customary tip-off. We can think of no coin and no stamp that has ever been "recalled"; the closest was the five-cent error of 1917, the sale of which was stopped when it was discovered.

When the Jefferson nickel appeared, it bore on the obverse Jefferson's home at Monticello. The building never boasted a flagpole, but the "get-rich-quick" suckers flocked to banks to get as many as they could. One heard on all sides, "It will be recalled; they forgot to put the flagpole on it."

More recently a new design for the common Lincoln penny appeared. In the legend, "United States of America," the first letter of the preposition, simply for the sake of artistry, was made smaller than all of the other letters. There were some days when we received as many as a dozen phone calls from fortunate possessors of this rare error soon to be recalled. To each of them the answer was given: "We'll pay you $10,000 for any that you can bring in without the small 'o.'"

People don't want to be told that what they want to believe is not true. More than a few insisted we didn't know what we were talking about.

Our plight was perhaps more enviable than that of the superintendent of coinage in Washington. Coming home one evening, he was greeted by his young daughter who had heard that day in school that the new Lincoln penny had an error on it, that it was to be recalled, and that it was going to be extremely rare. Fresh from a hectic day of denials at his office that such was the case, he advised his daughter that he, as superintendent of coinage, could assure her that there was absolutely no truth to the rumor.

"Oh, what do you know about it anyway?" replied the daughter, with the conviction that any parent encounters when he tries to reason with his progeny, when some preconceived notion of theirs conflicts with fact, logic, or reason.

Philately is even more rife with examples of similar rumors. Oddly enough, some of them have actually affected stamp values.

The Pony Express stamp issued in 1940, Scott #894, was one of those. The quantity in which it was issued, no less than 46,497,400, should not justify its present catalogue valuation of fifty cents each. There are many, many stamps issued in one-fifth the quantity that today list for considerably less. But the Pony Express stamp on its appearance received the same type of misleading publicity that the New York *Times* gave to the Glenn orbital stamp.

A national news agency quoted a world-famous sculptor as stating that no horse that ever lived could run in the position in which the pony shown on this stamp was holding, with one foot on the ground and three in the air. Turf enthusiasts joined the discussion, and letters to the editor appeared in newspapers from coast to coast from jockeys, from horse breeders, from veterinarians, and from anyone who considered himself sufficient authority on the subject to venture an opinion.

The descent on the post offices started, and the stamp collectors who paid little attention to the tale were left without their usual supply. By the time *they* descended on the post office, the stamps had been sold out, and they were replaced by the three-cent Pan-American issue, Scott #895. By this time the denials of the rumor that the Pony Express stamp was about to be recalled began to appear in the daily press, but not until the rumors began flying about that the Pan-American stamp, too, was about to be recalled, since it showed three young ladies in varying stages of disarray.

The misguided purchase of this stamp resulted in the same phenomenon: the stamp was soon sold out. Happily, by the time the next few commemoratives came along, sober thought ruled, or perhaps one could find nothing wrong with the capitol of the state of Idaho, pictured on Scott #896. But even today the large quantities of the Pony Express and Pan-American stamps taken from the usual philatelic channels affect the price. True, they now sell for much less than they did in the boom that followed their disappearance, but although issued in far greater quantities than some later commemoratives, they sell for immeasurably more.

Lest our remarks about philatelic misinformation as carried in the daily press be misconstrued, let us hasten to assure our readers that insofar as the stamp columns and stamp pages that appear in many papers are concerned, information in almost every case is correct and factual. As a rule, the stamp editors of almost every newspaper are well-informed men, practically and philatelically. What trouble does occur invariably comes from the mishandling of a philatelic news item by someone who is ill-equipped to pass upon it, and from the carelessness of a news editor in not submitting it to a person of philatelic consequence to pass upon it. In fact, as a philatelist, and seeing the woeful mishandling of so many items of philatelic news, we sometimes wonder how much else in the paper on other subjects may be factual.

Following the Pony Express and the Pan-American fiasco some years elapsed before rumor again supplanted reason in the issue of a stamp. In 1944 a stamp was issued to commemorate the seventy-fifth anniversary of the driving of the golden spike that completed work on the first transcontinental railroad. "The stamp will be recalled," the newspapers reported, "because it shows the wind blowing two ways at once. The smoke from the engine is blowing in one direction, while the flag is blowing in another." The Post Office Department explained the apparent inconsistency by saying that the flag was made to blow in the direction it did simply because if it blew in the same direction as the smoke it would be off the stamp. But, as usually happens, the denial never catches up with the story, or if it does, those who would rather not believe it choose not to listen.

Perhaps the greatest reversal of roles in two stamps occurred at least twice in philatelic history.

In 1899 the United States authorities in Cuba issued a special-delivery stamp for use in that recently freed country then occupied by American troops. The Spanish word for "immediate," by some odd circumstance, is "inmediata." An engraver in Washington, noticing the odd spelling, assumed that it was an error, and ignoring his instructions, he proceeded to engrave it "immediata."

Those aware of proper Spanish raised an outcry at this inexcusable error, and the buying rush started. Not only did philatelists rush to buy the stamp, but again the nonphilatelic public did as well. Uncle Sam willingly cooperated by keeping the supply going, so that no one had to be disappointed. When in 1904, by which time Cuba had its self-government, the stamp was reissued, bearing the proper spelling "inmediata," no one was interested. Today the correct version of the stamp is a much scarcer item than the error, which, because of the tremendous quantities in which it was bought, is today a very common item.

A similar incident happened in New Zealand.

That country issued a stamp picturing a large lake, with the inscription, "Lake Wailukupu." New Zealanders soon noticed that the name of the lake was grossly misspelled, and the rush to the post offices started. Vast quantities of it were sold, so many, in fact, that supplies ran out, requiring a new printing. In the new printing the name of the lake was spelled properly. Since it was only the error that interested the would-be opportunists, the newer stamp was more or less ignored. Today it, like the Cuban special delivery, is much more common in the error than in the corrected version.

Perhaps the most difficult rumors to squelch are those based on the quantities of a stamp in existence. Whenever a new series or even a single stamp appears, the less-informed philatelists, aided and abetted sometimes by those who should know better, discuss the chances for its appreciation in price. The fact that on far more occasions they have guessed wrong than right apparently does not discourage them one bit. It just simply is the case that the number printed has little to do with a stamp's subsequent market value.

In 1932 a set of twelve stamps was issued to commemorate the two hundredth anniversary of the birth of George Washington. It was the most ambitious philatelic commemoration since the Columbus and Omaha issues of almost forty years before, and all philately was agog. Columns appeared in the stamp magazines as to which value had the greatest possibilities for profit. Postage rates then in effect were analyzed, to determine which stamp would have the least use. The postage rate being two cents at the time, the two-cent, four-cent, and six-cent were immediately eliminated, since they would make multiples of the current rate. This took care of the eight-cent value as well. The ten-cent could be of no consequence, since this was the registry rate. The five-cent was of course the rate to Europe, while the two lowest values, the one-half-cent and the one-cent would have to be common, since they were issued to be used in connection with other values to make up various rates. As for the one-and-one-half-cent, everyone knew that this was the rate for circulars, so it would be issued in tremendous quantities. This left the seven-cent and the nine-cent.

The nine-cent happened to be a popular parcel-post rate at the time, so the smart boys, by the most logical process of elimination, centered on the seven-cent value. This, indeed, would be the one to wager would bring home the bacon. There was simply no rate at the time for which the seven-cent would be applicable, unless it were used in connection with other values. This is something which both the general public and post-office clerks are reluctant to do.

Of course, reference to a catalogue will disclose what happened. So many bought the seven-cent value that today sheets of it can be bought without any particular difficulty at a very modest advance over face value. And which stamps have been the winners in the bicentennial derby? They are the two which, according to all reason and all logic, should have been the most common, the six-cent (listing at eighty-five cents today) and the ten-cent, which no one thought even worthy of consideration. (Today it lists for $2.35!) Once again the wise ones had guessed wrong, and, in so doing, they had been followed by the mass of collectors who could not think for themselves.

If one concludes, though, that any lessons have been learned from this, then one is mistaken. We have sat in on many discussions among present-day collectors seeking to establish which of the eight-cent Champions of Liberty will lead the parade pricewise a dozen years from now. (None will, since all were printed in more than sufficient quantities to supply any conceivable demand, and all have been laid away in more than sufficient quantities to supply the market for many decades to come.)

When in 1934 another set was issued to commemorate National Parks Year, those who had not yet admitted defeat on their selection of the seven-cent Bicentennial as the prize stamp remained undaunted. Still pointing to the fact that the seven-cent Bicentennial had actually been issued in smaller quantities than any other value of that set, they concluded that the seven-cent Park had equal possibilities for speedy and substantial price appreciation. The suckers who follow every philatelic market tip hastened to place their bets on number seven. Again the information on which they acted was correct; of all values in the Parks series, the seven-cent was issued in the smallest quantity. But as was the case with the seven-cent Bicentennial, if one looks at it from the vantage of today's prices, the purchase was hardly a wise one. So many, in fact, bought it that today the allegedly scarce seven-cent value is the one value in the set that sells at a price closest to its face value. Rumor had again triumphed over logic.

The appearance of the Famous American issues of 1940 came at a most inopportune time insofar as philatelists were concerned. On such circumstances as these do the fates of an issue's future determine themselves. The country was just then emerging from the greatest depression in its history, with the economy awakening because of the great defense effort. Many collectors would have liked to have bought a set of sheets to put away, just as most of them had been buying sheets of other stamps of the same era. But $101.90, the face value of a set of sheets, was a lot of money. Even $5.88, the face value of a set of plate blocks, was a fair sum, and since obtaining a set at face value would mean at the very least thirty-five individual trips to the post office, the completion of a set was not an easy task. (Each of the thirty-five stamps came out on a different day, and not all post offices received supplies of all thirty-five stamps. Add to this the fact that one had to be in the post office the days the stamps were on sale, for supplies to any individual office were not large.)

Adding to the turmoil was the fact that 1940 was a year of crucial significance in the lives of a million or more collectors. Although the nation was not yet at war, the entire economy was being put on a war footing, and, more to the point, hundreds of thousands of young men were being drafted into the army. Popular though the Famous Americans were, they were of necessity completely neglected by many collectors who under normal circumstances would have bought them. The handwriting on the wall was there for all to read, but the smart money was still talking Pony Express. Yawns and indifference seemed to greet each new value of the Famous Americans, and when the final one appeared, the ten-cent Bell, Scott #893, there seemed to be little interest in it. The time seemed right to exercise one of the first laws of successful "investing": don't follow the crowd. Buy when people are not buying. We found an idle $100 and bought one thousand ten-cent Bells, all in complete sheets. It was one of our most lucrative purchases, especially since within five years the stamp had increased in price from ten cents each to $3.00 each.

The war boom created prosperity in the nation where there had been depression before. Those not in the service clamored for sets of Famous Americans. The lower values, the one-cent, two-cent, and three-cent values were freely available; some were still available in some post offices two or three years after the issue's original appearance in 1940. But since the demand was for the complete sets of thirty-five stamps, even if one were fortunate enough to find the lower values at face value, he still had to pay a stiff premium for some of the higher values. Those who had neglected to buy the last stamps issued paid well for their folly; not only the ten-cent Bell turned out relatively scarce, but its companion, the five-cent Howe, Scott #892, proved to be the scarcest of the five-cent values.

As the war ended, millions of servicemen returned to their homes, and to peaceful pursuits, to find that many of the stamps that had appeared during their absence, and which they had, of course, found it impossible to purchase, were obtainable only at large premiums. But money now was a good deal easier than it had been; high-salaried jobs were available for the asking. This tremendous buying power naturally concentrated on the Famous Americans, and the price of the complete set zoomed. The greatest increase was in the very values needed to complete sets, especially the ten-cent values. Here was a prime "investment," for the basic laws of economics applied: a small supply, a great demand.

The stage was set for a repetition of what has happened so often in philately. A new set was announced in 1944, and in the next several months, well into 1945, a series of thirteen stamps bearing the flags of thirteen nations conquered and occupied by the Axis powers appeared. The number of sets that were issued was quite limited. Less than fifteen million appeared; the number was not a random choice. It coincided approximately with the smallest number that had appeared of any of the 1940 Famous Americans. The Post Office had wisely limited the issue to the number they felt would sell readily. There was no purpose in having huge quantities left unsold, to be ultimately destroyed, as had happened twice with the Graf Zeppelin issues a few years before.

Times were different. Everyone was buying Occupied Nations stamps. Popularly called the "Flags," since each of the thirteen stamps bore the flag in color of the occupied nation being honored, the buying was stimulated. "Investors" were not content with buying individual sheets. The great amount of money in circulation, much of it "hot money" (the result of black-market operations), soon cleaned out the post offices. The Flags were issued in packages of 100 sheets each, each "pad" or "book," as it was called, having a face value of $250. One could buy a complete set of books, with comparative ease, despite the face value of $3,250. Many did.

The price of the Flags zoomed as did the Famous Americans of a short time before. But the circumstances were hardly the same. The 1940 set was in demand because there were few available; the Flags were in demand because of an artificial shortage, caused by huge supplies being temporarily withdrawn from the market. It is important in stamps to differentiate between a legitimate shortage caused by limited existing supplies and one caused by speculative buying.

In 1946 a set of Flag sheets, with a face value of $32.50, could be sold with ease for double face value of $65.00.

"Just wait until normal communication with these occupied nations is possible," the wise ones said. "Every collector in France is going to want a stamp with his country's flag on it. The same will be true of each of the other twelve stamps, for Denmark, for Austria, for the Netherlands, and for the others." To a certain extent this was true. Although Britain, to conserve its limited currency, was on a strict stamp embargo insofar as the importation of foreign stamps in that country was concerned, a few stamp dealers, who put their personal greed above their country's welfare, smuggled the Flag stamps into Britain. Those who were unable to smuggle out of Britain the dollars and pounds to pay for them paid for them with mint British and British Colonial stamps on a barter basis.

The illicit movement of stamps between Britain and this country reached such proportions, and created such consternation among the British dealers, that the office of censorship which had been established in Bermuda to open and censor civilian correspondence turned its attention primarily to philatelic mail. All letters proceeding in either direction containing stamps had their contents confiscated by a prize court there. One British dealer who tried to circumvent the censorship by proceeding direct to Bermuda to post the stamps to the United States from there was arrested as he stepped on the plane at London airport.

After the war, when the prize court decided to sell its huge stock of confiscated stamps, it announced a stamp auction in Bermuda. Both Britain and Bermuda claimed ownership of the fabulous hoard, but the latter established its claim. The auction lasted a week. Most of New York's dealers attended the sale. Just how many went with a sincere desire to buy stamps and how many went to enjoy the warm Bermuda sun and the lovely sand beaches will never be known, but Uncle Sam footed the bill for many a Bermuda vacation.

The promised demand from each of the occupied countries for its stamps did not materialize, nor is this surprising if one will analyze the situation. Several countries before the war had issued stamps in tribute to the United States, among them China, Ecuador, and Honduras. Each of these emissions was beautifully done, with a magnificent reproduction of the Stars and Stripes in full color. By and large, these lovely stamps were ignored by American collectors. Similarly, the French, Danish, Austrian, Dutch, and other collectors ignored our Flag stamps issued in their honor.

The bubble burst. The price of Flag sheets toppled. Within a relatively short time it was just half what it had been during the boom. Some of the more common varieties, of which the largest quantities had been issued (Belgium, the Netherlands, Luxembourg), actually sold below face value. Even the allegedly scarce ones, some issued in a quantity of less than fifteen million stamps (Greece, Denmark, Korea) dropped to prices not much above face value. The set has never recovered in price, nor is it likely to. It is now almost twenty years since the issue appeared. One can buy a complete set of sheets now for a modest percentage over the original face value.

Those who are today buying vast quantities of our current commemoratives in complete sheets can profit by the Flag experience if they wish to. It is unlikely that they will, however. Today's commemoratives are being issued in a quantity of from one hundred million to two hundred million. Uncle Sam is still gauging the demand quite accurately and, equally obligingly, is supplying the speculators with as many stamps as they are willing to buy.

The lesson should be apparent to the thinking buyer. There are two kinds of scarcity, one kind the result of a short supply and a great demand, the other the result of what may perhaps be a greater demand, but not accompanied by a short supply. It does not take more than average intelligence to differentiate between the two. The buyer who does has taken a long step toward "investing" wisely.

One need not devote any space to tell a philatelic "investor" how to take a profit once he has one. The ability of the human mechanism to adjust to a situation of this sort is phenomenal. However, it is a somewhat different matter when the stamp buyer is faced with the situation of deciding whether or not to take a certain loss. The invariable answer to a circumstance of this sort is to sit tight and wait for conditions to change. They seldom do.

Milton Ozaki of Littleton, Colorado, operates an "investment service" in connection with the systematic purchase of foreign stamps and sets, one of the few services of this sort that combine common sense with cold economic factors, and which, as a result of this, has achieved some satisfactory results for his clients. (It is possible under certain circumstances to have the pleasures of collecting with the satisfaction that one is buying advantageously, but it can't be done on the helter-skelter basis that so many uninformed collectors use.)

Ozaki recently advised his clients that one of the most difficult decisions to make in philately is what to do with stamps that they had purchased before "learning the basic principles of investment."

"My advice is hard to take," he continued, "but it's sincere: get rid of it in any way you can, even at a loss. It is my conviction that a bad buy is a bad buy, and that it's foolish to sit around hoping that some idiot will come along and pay you a high price for it. As long as you hang on to it, your money will be idle. Get rid of the bad buy, put the money into something good, and with any luck at all you'll not only recoup your loss, but you'll make a profit."

It has been said that there are only two prerequisites for anyone to become a philatelic columnist: an ability to write passable English, and a typewriter. This is not exactly correct; we know of a number of writers, some with a surprising following, who do not possess a typewriter.

Back in the late 1940s one of these made a prediction in *Mekeel's Stamp News.* He needed a fairly large quantity of two-cent stamps for a mailing for the church of which he was pastor. His local office advised him that there being such a limited demand for a two-cent stamp, none were in stock. They advised that he use two one-cent stamps. Being a New Englander, he tried the largest nearby post office, that of Manchester, New Hampshire. He found only a few odd sheets. They advised him to try Boston. Boston could do little better, although they suggested that if he needed a substantial supply, they would try Washington.

He was not long in getting to print: The lowly two-cent Presidential of 1939, a stamp that the speculators had completely ignored, was the coming rarity; just try to buy one at your local post office. It isn't known how many were impressed by the conclusion, but other magazines soon picked up the tip. After all, this is the news that most readers seemed to want. The refutations were not long in coming. They ranged from observations of those who were familiar with Post-Office policy, which has never distributed denominations for which there was little demand, to official statements from the Post Office itself, which stated quite unequivocally that there was little chance that a stamp of such low denomination, and part of a set at that, would be discontinued. But by then the columnist was off on another tangent, suggesting that the three-cent Discharge stamp, Scott #940, was going to prove to be rare since, being a small-sized stamp, the "investors" had neglected it in favor of the more popular large-sized commemoratives.

This last observation, which we refer to as the "small commemorative syndrome," is one that periodically recurs. We first recall it at the time of issuance of the 1933 NRA stamp, Scott #732. The fallacious reasoning was the same: speculators prefer the large stamps. And since few buy the small ones, because of their physical resemblance to regular issues (which do not have the quantities to be printed announced beforehand), the hand of Fate has to point profitably to such an issue. One heard the same chant when the Al Smith stamp (Scott #937) appeared, and with the NATO stamp (Scott #1008). We shall hear it again with each recurring small-sized commemorative. Needless to say, it isn't true, for the simple reason that *all* commemoratives of recent vintage are being bought in sufficiently large quantities to assure an adequate supply for the future. It is only when they are *not* bought, for one reason or another, and when the supply issued is likely to be less than the ultimate demand, that an issue has profit-making possibilities.

There is another phenomenon in stamp "investing" which defies all logic but which possesses so many stamp buyers that it cannot be dislodged from their minds. This we call the "face-value syndrome." It is simply that if one buys stamps at face value, he cannot possibly lose. As soon as he pays a premium for something, no matter how small, he is assuming an unjustified risk that can cause the loss of his "investment."

There is a rational explanation for this peculiar belief. Everyone likes to buy at wholesale. Most of us boast of our friends who can supply us with any needed item at a lesser price than the next man will have to pay. (We are reminded of a collector of whom a British dealer once told us. In the days when bargains were available in United States stamps in the British market, this party made the rounds of the London dealers, with a printed business card, intended to certify to his professional status. Printed on it, in order to emphasize that he wished to buy only at the lowest possible price, he had written, "We are wholesalers who wholesale to wholesalers." It was an apt expression, even if it did not serve to impress.)

There is an added consideration. The face value of a stamp may be regarded as a base, as a floor, below which the price cannot drop. (The fallacy of this is only too evident, much as the uninformed buyer chooses to ignore it.) By buying as close to this base as possible, he somehow feels that the possibility of loss is mitigated.

Last, there is yet another explanation. In the stamp field more than any other the buyer appears reluctant to allow the legitimate merchant a profit on his investment. He will buy his groceries from his chosen grocer without ever quibbling at the price, knowing that the difference between cost and market is the grocer's margin of living. He can understand when he buys his shoes that the shoe dealer is entitled to a markup on his merchandise. He can even realize that the years of training and study entitle his doctor to charge a fee that may bear little relation to the time taken to make a diagnosis or the cost of the medicine prescribed to relieve the ailment. But when a stamp dealer attempts to sell him a sheet of stamps of ten or twenty years ago at 10 per cent or 20 per cent over its original face value, he may balk at the purchase.

At a bourse at one of the recent stamp exhibitions a stranger approached our booth, showing ten sheets of a just-issued commemorative. "What do you think it will sell for in a year?" he asked.

"Not much more than you paid for it," we replied.

"But how can I lose? There were only 110,000,000 of them issued."

"Look at it this way. We can sell you sheets of commemoratives issued as far back as twenty-five years ago. On some of these as few as 35,000,000 were issued—one-third the quantity of the one you have just bought. In those intervening years millions have been used up, lost, discarded. When they appeared, few people were 'investing' in stamps. Yet you can buy some of these for as little as twenty-five cents per sheet over face value. If these haven't gone up in price, what chance is there for the one you just bought to make your purchase a profitable one?"

The chap was not impressed. He would be glad to pay the Post Office its price for a sheet of stamps, but the prospects of paying someone else a profit for a sheet of stamps was inconceivable. Little did he know that the poor soul who had originally bought that sheet a quarter century ago was not even destined to get his original investment back!

Of course there have been stamps issued in that time which have done handsomely for those fortunate enough to have bought them. The irony is that the ones which have returned handsome rewards are precisely the ones which the greater number of speculators failed to buy for one reason or another. Despite the Famous Americans, the five-cent Chinas (Scott

#906) and the handful of others which are today worth substantial premiums, the man who has purchased one sheet of every commemorative issued since 1935 at face value will not be able to get his money back; the premium on the better ones could not possibly offset what he will lose on the far greater number which have not increased in price.

Not long ago we advertised in one of the leading magazines a "collection" of mint sheets. It consisted of a sheet of *every* commemorative issued since 1927. It included such rare sheets as the Burgoyne (Scott #644), the Hawaiis (Scott #647 and #648), as well as the Bicentennials of 1932, the Famous Americans of 1940, and many others. The face value was close to two thousand dollars, and for the entire assortment we asked just 10 per cent over the face value. There were no takers, simply for the reason that perhaps 95 per cent of the sheets included were relatively common ones, easily obtainable at face value, or even at a slight discount. It was a great deal more effort, but we finally sold the lot by disposing of the rarer sheets at substantial premiums and selling the more common ones at a discount.

The sale of mint United States postage stamps at a discount from face value is really big business. If one picks up any stamp magazine he will see ads of postage brokers offering to buy mint stamps at a small discount. The discount varies with the denomination and with the type of stamp. One can sell complete sheets of stamps of whatever denomination is the then-current rate for as little as 3 per cent or 4 per cent below face. The higher (and less-used) the denomination, the higher the rate of discount. Since air-mail and special-delivery stamps cannot be used to pay ordinary postage rates, these may be subject to even greater discounts. There are some stamps, such as the special handling stamps, which will not bring more than half the original face value on the discount market.

The supply of stamps for these brokers seems to be never

ending. Stamp dealers supply a good many of them. Disgusted speculators supply even more. When a dealer buys a large collection of stamps, invariably there is an accumulation of mint sheets among them. While the price received by the collector selling the lot may be acceptable, the dealer, nevertheless, is confronted with the problem of disposing of that portion of it for which he has no sale. The aforesaid "face-value syndrome" precludes his selling many of these to speculators. There is far more than he can ever use on his own mail. Tucking them in the safe for ten or twenty years on the chance that they will improve in price is unwise; buying United States savings bonds would return a greater dividend. All that he can do is to discount them and thus divert them into postage channels. The process goes on every day. Theoretically, every time a philatelic holding of mint sheets is diverted into nonphilatelic commercial channels, it should make the remaining philatelic supply that much better in profit possibilities. It doesn't work that way. The supply of mint sheets is so vast that it is not likely ever to be absorbed. Those same 1935 commemoratives printed in such limited quantities are still available with ease at a tiny percentage over face value; if they have not yet been absorbed, what chances are there for the more recently issued stamps which continue to glut the market?

Uncle Sam points to the many millions of dollars of sheets of stamps which he sells to collectors annually, happily boasting that this is pure profit to him. It costs perhaps a dime a thousand to print these stamps; if they are of four-cent denomination, he obtains $40.00 per thousand. This is a most satisfactory markup, especially since his costs of doing business are negligible. The buyer even pays the registry postage to have them delivered. But there are no figures, nor will there ever be, which can tell how many of these stamps at some later date, maybe years later, are sold into postage channels, and the Post Office required to perform the service for which they were originally issued. What scant recompense there is lies in the fact that Uncle Sam has had the use of the speculator's money, interest free, for the period between the time of original purchase and the appearance of each stamp on a letter.

But let us not be too hard on the speculator. Even if we cannot feel too much sympathy for his misguided enthusiasm and his rather naïve belief that he is a philatelist, he is making it possible for tomorrow's generation of collectors to have an ample supply of stamps which they can buy at moderate prices. For proof of this, just study the prices of some of our very early commemoratives, many of them issued not in the hundreds of millions, but in the billions. Many of these sell for as much as fifty times the original face value. Why? Simply because the speculators were not around then to buy them.

Let's call forth a test of the reader's intelligence. Which would be the better buy in today's market: a stamp issued perhaps sixty or seventy years ago, selling for fifty times face value, and which in time can only grow scarcer, or a stamp at face value, issued yesterday, which is destined to be available at face value indefinitely into the future?

Rumor and sentiment can sometimes reach the stage of hysteria. No better example of this ever occurred than the fever pitch of excitement that coincided with the sale of the stamp "collection" of the late President Roosevelt.

The word "collection" is intentionally in quotation marks for this was no collection in the accepted sense of the word. It was an accumulation, including just about everything that F.D.R. could lay his hands on, by purchase or by gift or by seizure. Thousands of covers bearing a small fortune in foreign stamps, all addressed to the Department of State in Washington, found their way into his holdings. Original drawings, proofs, essays, sketches of proposed stamps which had been in

Post Office archives were appropriated for his personal collection.

When the late President was bored with looking at his stamps, he would start signing his name to every album, often on the album page itself. There is no way of knowing whether he did this in order to assure that when his collection would ultimately be sold it would bring a greater price, but obviously this is precisely what happened. He made full use of the facilities of the Bureau of Engraving and Printing to obtain luxurious morocco-leather gold-inscribed albums for his stamps, each bearing the presidential coat of arms. His foresight in building up a philatelic estate was incredible, even if it was not commendable.

Never before had a stamp collection belonging to a figure of Roosevelt's stature been sold, and philatelists and nonphilatelists alike were on the scene to obtain their share. Many others were represented by agents at the series of auctions. The original appraisal of the collection was made by the late George B. Sloane, an eminent authority, for many years a consultant on philatelic matters to insurance companies, estates, and probate courts. He estimated the value at $80,000, the greater part of which proved to be in material which Roosevelt had assumed possession of through means hardly designed to do prestige to the office which he held. The price which the estate brought when the last stamp had been sold was roughly three times that figure.

A pair of tweezers ostensibly belonging to the President brought $500. Practically speaking, they appeared no different from the ones used by the average collector, obtainable from any dealer for about thirty-five cents. His copy of the Scott catalogue, at least authenticated by his signature (his ingenuity failed him when he found himself unable to autograph those tweezers), brought several hundred dollars. But most incredible of all, lot after lot of the most ordinary stamps in the world, some so common that they were actually philatelically valueless, brought high prices, simply because they had reputedly belonged to F.D.R. For years thereafter single stamps of minimum catalogue value, mounted on tiny printed squares certifying as to their origin, were advertised at $1.00 each, then seventy-five cents each, finally twenty-five cents each. One still occasionally encounters them in wholesale auctions where they sometimes bring $10.00 per hundred. Collections frequently come on the market with one entire page devoted to a single stamp "from the President Roosevelt collection."

Sentiment can indeed be an expensive luxury, but in philately it pays not to be influenced by rumor or sentiment.

6. *Beware of pitfalls that trap the unwary.* The exercise of due care when the spending of money is concerned is always indicated.

A person may cross the street against the traffic lights, dart in between fast-moving cars, always taking it for granted that every driver is not only in complete command of his vehicle, but that his skill is such that he can successfully maneuver it around a dozen pedestrians, dashing hither and yon. That same pedestrian a few moments later, who trusted his very life to the skill of unknown drivers, will count his change twice when buying a newspaper and look askance at each coin lest it be counterfeit.

The same thought and care should be given when contemplating philatelic investments. Admittedly, it is difficult to resist some of the blandishments contained in the advertisements, or even in the stamp dealers' windows. The Securities and Exchange Commission polices Wall Street admirably well. In suggesting the sale of a bond, a dealer by law is not even permitted to guarantee that the next interest payment will be made. There is, unfortunately, no S.E.C. for the stamp trade. The gullibility of the customer is the only limit for extravagant claims.

For years the diamond dealers have been perpetrating a huge fraud on the buying public with the constantly repeated slogan,

"Buy Diamonds for Investment." It has, in fact, been repeated so often that there are many people who today believe it. Just what the investment can be in a field where there are several markups between manufacturer and retailer, and where, to top it all, one has to pay a stiff tax on the retail price, is something that has always escaped us.

The very artificiality of the diamond market, with its international cartels, its rigged prices, and its controlled market may in one way be a guarantee of safety of principal, but as a general rule an investor is much safer betting his dollars in a field where the time-honored rules of supply and demand prevail.

If one has ever tried to sell a diamond bought ten or twenty years before, he will soon learn what a wonderful investment diamonds can be, once the very harsh hand of fashion takes command. A customer once impressed us with a huge three-carat stone that to our inexperienced eye seemed the acme of desirability. "Can't sell it," he said, "unless I spend $400 getting it recut and reducing the size. They called it an 'old miner.'"

An "old miner," as it turned out, is a diamond cut according to the fashion of another day, and today about as salable at a good price as a gold-plated buggy whip.

We bring in the matter of diamonds for a very good reason, as it brings a very good point to mind.

Since we have established that the stamp collector is in essence buying at retail when he buys, and that he has to sell at wholesale when he sells, his chances of making money are greatly increased by reducing the spread between wholesale and retail. This spread can be reduced in several ways.

Through a lucky purchase, perhaps because of superior knowledge, or even through buying from an uninformed seller, he may be able to buy at a price so much below retail that he can immediately sell at wholesale at a profit. This happens often enough so that it is not unusual, but it is not given to those who

77

possess neither good luck nor knowledge. (We have already dealt with the need for knowledge in stamp buying; unfortunately, we know of no method by which we can suggest that our reader become lucky.)

The more frequent way of buying at retail and being able to sell profitably is to anticipate an increase in price of such extent that the conventional buying price will be higher than the cost price. This, of course, is the dream of every stamp investor, and this is generally what occurs. All things being equal, the constantly increasing number of collectors and the constantly decreasing supply of a given stamp will produce an ascending curve representing value. But for this all things must be equal. An artificially stimulated market, rigged pricing, incorrect information, or simulated demand may give the appearance of an increased price, without the basis needed to bring it about, i.e., sincere buyers.

These rigged markets occur in philately more often than collectors realize. They cannot occur in issues of stamps that are genuinely scarce and in considerable demand. They cannot occur among stamps that are so diversified in ownership that no one individual, or group of individuals, can control the greater part of the existing supply, or even the floating supply. This leaves one field wide open for manipulation: the field of modern stamps and new issues.

Manipulated issues are nothing new. At the end of the last century Nicholas Seebeck, a New York stamp dealer, made a simple proposition to a number of South and Central American countries. All he wanted to be able to do was to pay the full costs of printing stamps for the nations which accepted his proposition. He would supply all their postal needs, and all he wanted in exchange was the unsold portion of each issue when it was to be retired, and the plates from which it had been printed.

In those earlier days of philately, even though collectors and dealers screamed to the high heavens about the iniquities of the deal, most countries to whom even the cost of printing an issue of stamps was a demand on the treasury to be avoided if it could be, found it difficult to decline the proposition. The list of those falling in with Seebeck's plan was a long one: Ecuador, Honduras, Nicaragua, among others. (It is noteworthy that at least in this instance philatelic memories are long ones. The Seebeck countries never again have achieved complete philatelic acceptability. Those which successfully resisted, such as Guatemala, maintained their respectability.)

Today it is different. Seebeck is gone, but in his place there now are cultured, polished gentlemen, offering the finest of philatelic workmanship from the world's most esteemed stamp engravers. But the basis of the scheme is the same.

In March 1962, at a stamp show in London, we had the pleasure of meeting the chief of the Philatelic Section of the Netherlands Post Office, J. J. M. Kiggen. The Netherlands has always maintained its respected name in the world of philately.

"Regularly, every six months they come," my friend said. "I call them 'the ambassadors,' for they dress like delegates to the United Nations. But the proposition is always the same: if I will only sign on the dotted line to let them 'represent' me in New York, or if I will let them dictate and control the stamp issues they propose, they will make it well worth my while. My answer is always no, but six months later the ambassadors will call again, I know."

The list of countries which have put themselves into the hands of philatelic groups grows larger. The nations of Africa that have achieved independence in recent years have almost uniformly sold themselves out for the rewards involved. Some of these, such as Ghana, have exploited the collector to such an unmerciful degree that it is simply unbelievable that collectors of Ghana stamps keep coming back for more.

Other countries, such as Switzerland, Israel, and West Germany, also maintain philatelic agents in New York, but at least they conduct their activities with full recognition of the amenities of collecting. Favoritism, kickbacks, rigged prices, made-to-order "errors" are avoided like the plague.

Still other nations, such as Monaco, Liechtenstein, and Luxembourg, all of whom find the issuance of attractive stamps and the maintenance of philatelic respectability a very good substitute for taxes, simply make use of the services of respected dealers in the United States and abroad for the distribution of their stamps.

The African countries particularly have gone all out to force their wares into the albums of the unwary. They are beautiful stamps for the most part; they are brightly colored and well executed. The collector who buys them for their philatelic value, or to maintain a collection of new issues, has every reason to be happy about his purchase. The one who buys them thinking that he is making a desirable philatelic investment is in all probability going to be greatly disappointed.

It is far from difficult to rig the price of a stamp issue when you control the existing supply as well as the means of distribution. It is done almost daily. Simply announce that an issue will be on sale for only thirty days, unless sold out sooner. Stop the sale and pronounce the stamps sold out after three weeks. Dealers will be only too happy to raise their prices on the supplies outstanding. Reward personal friends and steady buyers with supplies that have been held off the market; you will be surprised how close-mouthed a dealer can be when he is on the inside of a deal of this sort. Distribute your surplus carefully on a rising market; it is up to you whether you should increase your own prices or not as the market rises. Then when you are sold out pass along to another issue. If prices collapse, that's unfortunate. You can always say that speculation in stamps is a bad thing. And after all you warned your public that the issue was only to be on sale a limited time, "until sold out," the announcement read. Your hands are clean, and meanwhile there is a new issue coming up, this time with a souvenir sheet thrown in to ensnare those who stayed out last time.

When Castro took power in Cuba, he was not in control a month before his representatives were in New York seeking to make a deal with stamp firms for handling the stamps he planned to issue. The only thing that prevented conclusion of the deal was that his representatives pressed too hard and demanded a larger clandestine reward for themselves than anyone was able to give.

When a leader of a certain newly independent African republic came to this country to address the United Nations, the equally cogent reason for his coming was a reception for the stamp dealers in the United States who had done such a successful job in marketing his stamps that his personal philatelic income from the sale in all probability exceeded the salary he received as chief of state.

The outstanding social event of the philatelic season insofar as the stamp trade was concerned in 1961 was a reception for stamp dealers at a luxurious downtown New York hotel, with sufficient supplies of imported champagne to satisfy even the most thirsty. Within days of that meeting was another for philatelic writers, sponsored by another African republic. A souvenir of that meeting was a newly-issued stamp, printed and distributed only for this select group. Obviously, it will never merit catalogue recognition, but specialists in that country's stamps will always be prospects for it. Before the party ended, some of the writers had sold their souvenirs for prices reported to be $20.00 and more.

But this kind of activity is not by any means the new issue field.

For every country that indulges in these shenanigans there are dozens that refuse to allow themselves to be prostituted.

As a general rule, one can usually guess in which camp any nation will find itself. At the top of the ladder of philatelic respectability are the Anglo-Saxon and English-speaking nations, notably the United States, and Great Britain and its dominions. Whereas until comparatively recent times British colonies could be found with the mother country; many of them, having tasted of independence in political action, have found it difficult to follow in the footsteps of the mother country in the philatelic field.

Italy, under Mussolini, sold out its good philatelic name by demonetizing its stamp issues and then redistributing withheld supplies at prices considerably under the original face value. After the war Italy was partly restored in the good graces of collectors, only to fall even deeper than it had thirty years ago by announcing that it planned to sell supplies of stamps it had found in its archives, going back almost a century. (It is heartening to note that the disgust that this announcement generated was so great that, when the auction was held, no dealer cared to bid even the minimum amount that the Italian government had set as its first bid. At last word, though, the Italian government was investigating other channels of possible sale.)

Hitler in Germany found stamps a most useful vehicle for lining his pockets and that of his friends. Each year a set of stamps was issued allegedly for charity, called the Winterhilfe issue. Each stamp carried two denominations, one being the amount for which it was valid for postage, the second sum being the amount destined for charity. The stamp was sold at the post office for the sum of the two amounts. Not a *pfennig* of any issue went for charity, but stamp collectors in Germany found it was their patriotic duty, nevertheless, to buy the stamps.

When Hitler seized Austria, he found in the Austrian State Printing Office the original plates that had been used to print various Austrian stamps. Shortly before *Anschluss* Austria had issued a ten-schilling stamp picturing Chancellor Dollfuss. One of Hitler's first acts concerning Austria was to have Dollfuss murdered; he then forbade the use of any stamps bearing his portrait. Overnight hundreds of Engelbert Dollfussplatzes from one end of the country to another became Adolf Hitlerplatzes, as Austrians hastened to bow to their new tyrant. But Hitler, not to honor the Dollfuss memory, but merely to profit from it, was reprinting the ten-schilling Dollfuss stamp for sale to collectors in neutral countries and abroad. The fact that it is still a very rare and valuable stamp, despite the reprinting (which, incidentally, cannot be told from the original), only gives indication of the great rarity that it might have been had Hitler not reprinted it.

One way to gauge the decision whether or not to buy a given country's new issues is to look into the manner in which the collectors of the nation concerned accept their own stamps.

As a general rule, stamps that are extremely popular in the country of issue will be similarly popular all over the world. If there is little or no demand for the stamps in the issuing country, the red flag is up and the collector would do well to think twice before climbing aboard.

If there are stamp collectors in Ghana, Liberia, Togo, and Mali, and there well may be, their numbers could not be too large. Certainly more of their stamps are sold in New York than are sold by all the combined post offices in each country. We cannot question that some of these countries may need stamps, although it does strike the observer as a bit ludicrous when a nation without either airplanes or airports nevertheless issues a complete set of air-mail stamps.

If a collector, knowing all these things, wishes to collect the stamps of a given country, there certainly should be no one to say him nay. Such a collection can be a thing of beauty, one that gives joy of possession and pride in display. Just woe betide the individual who feels that buying such material is an investment that is destined to pay him what are euphemistically called philatelic "dividends."

But there are other pitfalls ready to trap the unwary. Not the least of these are the beasts inhabiting the philatelic jungle looking for the fresh meat of those who are themselves looking for bargains.

The prize dope in philately is the man who feels that desirable stamps are available simply for the asking at less than they are worth. He is the same man who will buy a $10.00 bill for $8.00 without suspecting that it is counterfeit, or who will buy a $100 diamond from a street peddler for $10.00. He is blessed with such supreme confidence in himself that he simply feels that, because of his own good looks or his princely demeanor, the entire world is willing to supply him with his needs at a lesser price than anyone else would have to pay.

The stamp woods are full of buyers whose collections reflect the bargain-hunting proclivities of their owners, and the word "reflect" is used advisedly. As someone once said, "A bargain is a bargain, and always looks it."

If a stamp has an acknowledged value of $10.00, is it reasonable that any merchant would willingly sell it for $5.00, unless of course he was more interested in a sale than a profit? Whether or not we agree with the pricing policy of the Scott catalogue, if a given stamp is priced at $100 we could perhaps understand its being sold for $50.00 or $60.00 and, if not in the best condition, even $10.00 or $15.00. But dealers have never been able to understand how otherwise seemingly intelligent people will show with pride a stamp in apparently perfect condition, catalogue value $100, which some kind soul generously let them have for $5.00 or $10.00. Yet this happens more frequently than anyone could possibly realize.

Of course if one suggests to these sublime optimists that the bargain stamp may not be what it is purported to be, the usual response is that it is "guaranteed." The mere meaning of the word "guarantee" varies with many. Some dealers when guaranteeing a stamp to be genuine simply mean "prove to my satisfaction that it isn't genuine and I will refund your money." Squaring the circle might be a far less formidable task than proving the stamp not genuine. Others may offer a stronger guarantee that somehow is not remembered when the time comes to seek a refund on it.

In security investing there is a saying that well extends itself to stamps: a guarantee is no better than a guarantor. We have seen stamps in collections so patently manufactured, simulated, or faked that they would be unlikely to fool a knowledgeable juvenile, but the proud owner tries to refute the viewer's skepticism with the remark, "Of course it's guaranteed." If he is asked who the guarantor is, either he does not remember, or he will come up with the name of some gas-station operator turned stamp dealer whose guarantee on an inflated tire as to its pressure would carry considerably greater weight. A tribute to the high caliber of ethical stamp dealers is the fact that the number of questionable items obtained from top-flight dealers is limited indeed.

No ethical dealer would be reluctant to pencil lightly on the back his name and the identification of the stamp when requested to do so by a buyer. Such a "guarantee" would have far greater significance than a verbal assurance from an unqualified dealer whose certainty that the stamp was as represented may

85

have been momentarily blinded by the sum of money about to be paid for it. While such an individual might even be willing to sign a statement as to the genuineness of the stamp in question, the chances are that he would affect a pose of injured dignity, exclaiming that if his verbal assurance is not sufficient, the stamp need not be bought. It seldom fails to work; the possibility of losing such an astounding bargain is too great a risk to run, far greater, it would seem, than the chance that the stamp is not genuine.

If there is ever any doubt in the buyer's mind as to the identity, genuineness, or condition of a stamp, a written notation lightly penciled on the stamp is a legitimate expectation. If it is not willingly given, avoid the stamp like the plague. A written guarantee offered separately is equally acceptable, provided a photograph of the stamp accompanies, and there is no question that the stamp referred to in the guarantee is the one photographed. The trade still laughs about the crooked dealer who obtained a guarantee on a stamp and sold the guarantee with a fake stamp of similar appearance. Each time he received another order, he obtained a new guarantee, passing it along with another fake. As long as he continued to retain the genuine stamp, he had a very lucrative business. It ended when he got mixed up one day and sold the genuine. The next time he sought a guarantee, he was turned down, since all he had was the fake.

There is a collector in Oklahoma City whose goal is to have a complete collection of United States stamps. He has finally come within striking range of his objective, and, surprisingly enough, he has been most fortunate in accomplishing the task without the expenditure of as much money as one might think would be necessary. There is no question that he is proud of his collection, and when he shows it to friends we are certain they are suitably impressed.

Our Oklahoma friend, whom we shall call Bill Harsch, for that is not his name, has access to a printing press. Periodically he prints his want list, which is now down to about two dozen stamps, all of them great rarities. He plainly states on the list that he will not pay more than 35 per cent of the Scott catalogue prices. After all, why should he? He has had little trouble in building his collection this far, and he has never had to pay more.

Although we felt that it would be a waste of time, since bargain hunters don't like to be told that *they* are wasting *their* time, we wrote Harsch that almost any dealer would pay him two or three times his offered price for the very same items. His reply was prompt; he had just bought Scott #294 b, the one-cent Pan-American of 1902, with inverted center, and he had paid only $100 for it, a price a good deal less than 35 per cent of catalogue. To prove his point, he was glad to send it along, to prove that philatelic bargains were definitely available.

Mr. Harsch seemed to be more adept in setting type by hand than in examining stamps. It did not take an expert to see that someone had simply taken the center portion of another one-cent Pan-American stamp, and, placing it on top of the normal one, subjected it to pressure after first applying the glue. It certainly gave the appearance of being the rare invert, which catalogues at $1,150, but if one held it to the light, even a tyro could see that the center portion of the stamp was two thicknesses of paper, while the rest was just one thickness.

Mr. Harsch obtained his refund, but he accepted the explanation of his dealer that anyone could make a mistake. His most recent purchase was a splendid example of a very rare coil, Scott #316. On this stamp the Scott catalogue carries a warning to collectors to beware of simulated reproductions, which, of course, can be made by anyone combining the ability to wield a scissors properly, with a certain steadiness of hand. As a further measure not to encourage the swindling of the gullible, Scott declines to put a price on the stamp in used condition.

"I paid $25.00 for it," Mr. Harsch wrote, "and I'm sure it's genuine. I wonder if you would look at it and, if you agree, put your name on it."

We told Mr. Harsch that the last copy of the stamp that we recalled seeing sold at auction for $300, but then it had the guarantee of a reputable dealer accompany it. But then $25.00 for a stamp worth $300 seemed more in line with Mr. Harsch's buying policies, whether or not the stamp was authentic.

There are more Mr. Harsches in the stamp field than one can possibly realize. Were it not so, there would not be as many dishonest stamp dealers as there are. True, the dishonest ones are the tiniest minority of those in business. By and large, most dealers are honest businessmen, trying to serve the philatelic public to the best of their ability. There is little competition between ethical dealers, for there is ample business for all of them; what competition does ensue between dealers—and it sometimes calls for bitter denunciation of the unethical—is between the honest ones and those beyond the pale.

We have had otherwise intelligent collectors show us a stamp with the accompanying explanation, "Of course I know it's a fake. I'm no fool, and I know no one is going to sell me a $100 stamp for $5.00. But isn't even a fake for $5.00 a cheap way to fill the space?"

If it's a fake, even fifty cents would be too much. That space would look much better empty than filled with a counterfeit. Even a single fake in a collection stands out so prominently that anyone looking at it will naturally question other stamps in the collection which may actually be genuine.

Even aside from the matter of a guarantee on a stamp, the salability of a stamp may be increased or decreased according to the identity of the guarantor. The name "Mueller" on an Austrian stamp would carry the highest degree of reliability, while the name "Ashbrook" on a United States stamp would carry similar respect. We cannot conceive of Ashbrook guaranteeing an Austrian stamp, but were he to have done so, we are sure it would carry weight. Nevertheless, the name "Mueller" would be one that would be far less likely ever to be questioned on that particular stamp.

Many of the financial plans for profitable stamp buying suggest that in "investing" in stamps one can successfully build a hedge against inflation.

It is certainly true that the most fortunate individuals in any nation unfortunate enough to have suffered a runaway inflation were those who had an appreciable share of their fortune in postage stamps, especially if those stamps were the kind that had international acceptability. Those who put their trust in currency, or savings, or bonds, or stocks, soon found that they were wiped out. Those with merchandise on hand or even real estate were relatively more fortunate, but since none of these had the international acceptability of stamps, nor the relative ease with which they could be moved to another country, it was the possessor of stamps who came out best in the long run.

In the inflations that struck so many countries after both world wars, it was those who had appreciable amounts tucked away in stamps who could get off to a head start by selling them when the new currency came into vogue. Thousands of German refugees arrived in this country penniless, their money, their jewelry, their every possession confiscated, but with a handful of valuable stamps which they had smuggled out of Germany they could start life anew. Our book *Nassau Street* had many factual stories on these very lines.

It is quite unlikely that the United States will ever undergo a ruinous inflation. True, for two decades we have been subject to an inflation that has eroded the buying power of the dollar, although not to the extent where it has curbed buying power to any great extent. So we feel that the appeal to the public to buy stamps "as a hedge against inflation" is a rather weak appeal.

The inflation that we have undergone since the war is a moderate one, with the buying power of the dollar decreasing at perhaps 1 per cent or even 2 per cent per year. This adds up to a substantial sum over a period of years, but would investment in stamps have really proved a hedge?

Let us assume for the sake of argument that this country is due for a real inflation, one in which its currency will decline in buying power perhaps as much as 10 per cent in a single year. To protect against this you have decided to buy as many stamps as you can possibly buy, subject only to other more necessary demands on your finances. This could be $20.00 per week, perhaps more, but $20.00 will suffice for the purpose at hand. Twenty dollars a week is $1,040 per year—certainly a sum far in excess of what the average philatelist finds it possible to spend. Assuming that his stamps have not increased in price, but his money has decreased, his hedge against inflation has netted him exactly $104—hardly enough to keep him in cigarettes if he smokes much more than a pack a day.

These "hedge-against-inflation" plans that call for an investment of $5.00 or even $10.00 a week strike us as just so much malarkey. Better to call it a stamp budget, or a form of saving, than to ape the language of Wall Street and call it a hedge.

The collecting of stamps and the desire to mount them presentably in albums call for a certain amount of finger dexterity. As often as not this dexterity is accompanied by an ability to decorate the album pages in a creditable manner. We have seen many handsome pages; in fact, many times the bright colors and the art work on the pages actually surpass the artistry of the stamps themselves.

As long as the collector knows that his art work, whether he has done it himself or had it professionally done, is incidental to the value of the stamps, there is no harm done. But we have occasionally encountered collectors who in recounting how much their collection has cost them include in that price the cost paid to a professional artist for illuminating the pages in the style of the medieval scripture students. We know of one prominent collection of Israel stamps each page of which strives to reproduce a magnificent stained-glass window. The owner's boast is that he has paid $20.00 for the art work on each page, yet on some pages the stamps themselves are worth but fifteen or twenty cents. He has the entire collection insured for $25,000; we hope that he will never have a loss, for we foresee no little difficulty in his being able to convince the insurance company that his stamps are worth that sum, even if the collection may have cost him as much.

Many times a collector forced to sell his collection for one reason or another begs us to keep it intact. Understandably, he cannot bear the thought of seeing the stamps that he has so patiently and so carefully mounted ruthlessly torn from the sheets. If he has decorated or painted the pages in addition, the thought of seeing his many hours of effort desecrated is an unpleasant thing to contemplate. And yet it is the unpleasant task of the dealer to explain to him that seldom does anyone buy someone else's art work, at least in a stamp collection. It is the stamps that have value; a collector who would be inclined to want to own a tastefully decorated album would, in all probability, want either to do his own art work or to have it done according to his own taste and design.

It seems a shame to toss into the wastebasket some of the magnificently designed pages that have had to end up there, but long ago we learned that collectors do not like to buy collections intact, and that they will not pay for someone else's mounting efforts. Among the joys of collecting are those of accumulating a collection bit by bit, through one's own efforts, and if there is a need for hand decorating it, to do it one's self.

Probably the most expensively mounted collection in philatelic history was the air-mail collection of Dr. Philip Cole, a New York dentist, whose collection was sold some years ago following his death. The stamps themselves were a fabulous lot, since this was up to the time of Dr. Cole's passing probably the finest collection of air-mail stamps ever assembled in the world. Dr. Cole had mounted it in magnificent hand-tooled leather and gilt albums, each bearing his name. Reputedly, the albums alone had cost him more than twenty thousand dollars. They were offered in the same sale in which his stamps had brought such tremendous prices. Their selling price was but a mere fraction of their original cost, which, of course, was not the least bit surprising.

In collecting stamps the stamp is the thing. Whatever in cost is added to the value of the stamps, be it albums, stamp mounts, or art work, is just additional window dressing. When the collection is to be sold, such adjuncts should be charged to the personal satisfaction and pleasure which they may have brought. The prospective buyer is interested in buying only the stamps.

Does that part-time dealer whose office is his kitchen table give better buys than the chap with a full-time store? How about that nice chap whose stamp business is a one-man operation, perhaps occasionally assisted by his wife? Is he more likely to give better service than the man who occupies extensive space, with a staff of a dozen employees?

There is no certain answer to any of these questions. The reply depends too much on the individual. Many an individual entrepreneur of today is the colossus of tomorrow. Many dealers who could have been colossi had they so desired have remained small by design, in order to give what they felt to be better service.

There is too much unjustified condemnation of the part-time dealer. And yet virtually every successful dealer of stature himself started as a part-time dealer, the writer included. It takes a lot of guts to give up a full-time job, especially if one has earned a living from it for any period of time, in order to venture into a field which can be as unrewarding financially as stamps can sometimes be. And yet the desire, if not the ultimate intention, to be a stamp dealer lies strong in every philatelist's breast.

The closest we can come to answering the questions about the large dealer versus the small dealer is to make an observation that is certainly true in more cases than it is not. That is that the smaller, less-experienced dealer is more likely to overprice any really unusual item than the larger and more experienced dealer, who handles and sells rarities with such frequency that he is less likely to be awed by them.

Again we come back to the oft-repeated advice. The finest insurance that any collector can have against making a bad buy, in preventing his being taken advantage of, in assuring that his philatelic dollar buys everything that it should, is to enlighten himself on every phase of the stamps he is collecting and the market in which he finds himself. Only then can he be certain that he is getting for his money all that he is told he is obtaining.

In short, the informed collector will take steps to beware the pitfalls that trap the unwary.

7. *Rarity alone does not make value.* In past chapters it has been our intention to bring our reader's attention to the fact that the basic laws of supply and demand apply to stamps as they do to any other commodity in the market places of the world. The law can be tampered with by withholding merchandise from the market, or by maintaining an artificial price level, as is done with diamonds or certain issues of stamps. But given a free market, and allowing buyers and sellers to meet in the same market place, without arbitrary restrictions, prices will follow their natural bent.

But, as has been shown, it is only the interplay of supply and demand which establishes price. To return to the proverbial Eskimo and the refrigerator, it is not only the lack of demand that mitigates any business being done. Conceivably, there might be one Eskimo who would regard the purchase of a refrigerator as a status symbol, or as a useful device for storing blubber, but if he had no money to pay for it (i.e., no demand which could be translated into an ability to purchase), no transaction will result.

Ernest A. Kehr, stamp editor of the New York *Herald Tribune,* once pointed out that one of the rarest stamps in the world, of which but ten examples are known to exist, is a stamp issued by Italy for the use of its offices in China, a not particularly pulchritudinous adhesive surcharged "PECHINO 40

CENT," and used from 1901 to 1926. It is so rare that seldom is one available, but the last time one came up for sale at auction it brought the rather unprincely sum of $400. (In contrast, the famed twenty-four-cent 1918 United States air-mail stamp, with the airplane inverted, of which 100 originally existed, last sold for $9,200.)

As almost every philatelist knows, the most valuable stamp in the world—in fact, for its weight, allegedly the most valuable single item of any sort—is the British Guiana one-cent stamp of 1851, of which only a single example has come down to us. At one time there must have been an entire sheet of them, perhaps even more. The single example known, which, in passing, should be mentioned as being damaged, was bought by a tourist who visited Demerara, British Guiana, about eighty years ago, who chanced to ask a youngster on the dock where he might buy some stamps for his collection. The boy ran home and came back with a handful of odd items that he had been trying to do something with for some time. The tourist, Ridpath by name, an Englishman, offered the lad five shillings, and, taking the money hurriedly, the boy ran off, probably laughing to himself at the stupidity of an Englishman who thought so much of a few ugly scraps of paper.

Of course no other example ever turned up. Ridpath eventually sold it to a British provincial dealer, who in turn sold it to one of his customers. Its comparative rarity was not suspected for some time, for other examples of the same series, in other denominations, were known. In time the stamp found its way into the famed collection of Baron Ferrari, the world's outstanding and wealthiest collector in the first two decades of this century. Ferrari paid $500 for it.

The Ferrari family was of mixed European origin, especially Austrian, and although the baron lived in Paris, he took refuge in neutral Switzerland during World War I. After his death, the French government convinced itself that Ferrari was actually an enemy alien, and his collection, which he had somewhat foolishly left in France, was seized as enemy property, the proceeds to be applied to the reparations that France levied on its defeated enemies. The collection was sold in a series of auction sales in the early 1920s. It brought a price well in excess of one million dollars, up to that time the most valuable stamp collection ever sold.

By this time the unique status of the British Guiana one cent of 1851 was pretty well established. No second copy had ever appeared, even though in the intervening forty years countless tourists had boarded ship for Demerara and contacted every lad hanging around the dock, in quest of stamps. There was tension in the room when the British Guiana stamp came·up, for a new philatelic titan, Arthur Hind, of Utica, New York, was represented by an agent, and all knew that the Hind collection, at the time the world's largest, of course lacked the stamp.

Reputedly, although this has never been positively established, another agent in the room carried the instructions of an equally prominent philatelist, who was reported to have a virtually complete collection of British Colonial stamps, lacking this one specimen, of course. That philatelist was King George V of Great Britain, a former president of the Royal Philatelic Society of London, author of several competent monographs on stamps, and a philatelist in his own right in the full sense of the word.

When the bidding stopped on the stamp, the price had reached $22,500. The French government, not content with the net proceeds of the fabulous sale, levied a further tax on every purchase, so the total price paid was $27,500. The purchaser was Arthur Hind. If it had been King George's desire to add the stamp to his collection, his efforts had been in vain.

The stamp "that a king could not obtain" achieved a status

that few others had ever achieved. There are any number of stamps that are of a unique status, i.e., of which no other specimens exist, but because of the circumstances surrounding this one, from its original finding to its romantic final sale, it achieved an aura achieved by no other.

And why do we give so much space to the well-known and many-times repeated tale of the British Guiana one-cent? It is simply this: during the period in which Baron Ferrari owned the stamp there were others who sought to add it to their collections, among them a collector named Tapling, who had amassed the finest collection ever assembled by a Briton at any time. (This collection was subsequently donated by Tapling to the British Museum, where it is on public view today. It is the finest collection in the world in public hands.)

When Tapling found that all his offers to buy the stamp were declined by Baron Ferrari, he conceived the idea of a swap, whereby he would offer a stamp of equal rarity which he possessed, to which he would be willing to add other valuable considerations in the form of money and stamps. His prize possession was a stamp that had been issued by one of the many states of India. At one time some of these states possessed sufficient sovereignty, even as late as 1947 (in which year India achieved full independence) to issue their own stamps. The stamp was that of Poona. Even today it maintains its unique status. It is equally as rare as the British Guiana one-cent, being unique.

That Baron Ferrari rejected the proffered exchange is only incidental to the story. The point is that in the minds of eminent philatelists, and certainly in the opinion of Tapling, the Poona stamp was no more or less valuable than the British Guiana. Philatelists had the opportunity to reflect on this observation when in comparatively recent times the unique Poona stamp was sold at auction. It brought $500.

Rarity alone does not make value.

The stamp that a king could not buy is still the world's most precious bit of paper. When the Hind collection was sold, the stamp was held by Hind's widow, who claimed that it was a deathbed presentation to her and not part of the Hind collection, which, when sold at auction, brought almost two million dollars. The stamp subsequently sold privately for a sum reputed to be $37,500. Its present whereabouts is unknown. Today, the tax situation being what it is, millionaire stamp collectors no longer boast either of their acquisitions or their possessions, but occasionally the trade hears that the present owner or owners would not be unwilling to sell the ugly bit of magenta paper for $100,000.

The purists who maintain that a stamp must be in perfect condition qualify their contention when the British Guiana one-cent is discussed. Under certain conditions the fact that a stamp may be damaged is of little consequence. Other stamps that are held in equally high esteem are those primitive emissions of Hawaii, which were mostly used by the early missionaries to this then-heathen land. The stamps, bearing numerals as their central design, and popularly called "missionaries," were printed on a very thin fragile paper, so delicate, in fact, that although a few dozen are known, not a single one is known in other than damaged condition. Yet on the few occasions when they do come up for sale they invariably bring prices in the several thousands of dollars. It is also one of the more frequently counterfeited stamps that one encounters. As can be readily understood, most of the counterfeits are in perfect condition.

Counterfeits of rare stamps are not the insurmountable problem that one might think. It hardly pays to counterfeit relatively common stamps, although this does sometimes happen. The substantial rewards; however, are in the counterfeiting of the great rarities. But since all of the great rarities are pretty well pedigreed, and since the buyer of a great rarity generally possesses at least as much knowledge as the seller, the chances of successfully passing off a reproduction are rather remote. Among the monied collectors of the world there are few seekers of bargains, and only the bargain hunter would be likely to be fooled by the purchase of a stamp "just as good."

There are other factors peculiar to philately that would seem to confound the neophyte in philately. A keen demand for certain material without any accompanying available supply can result in a static market.

One popular phase of collecting, for example, is the field of used blocks of United States stamps.

On a number of relatively common United States stamps —and this includes many modern emissions—used blocks are seldom encountered. There are many, many of our stamps of which mint blocks are frequently seen. They may be expensive, because of their popularity and their comparative difficulty of purchase, but in used blocks they approach the point of rarities. Some of these may catalogue as little as a few dollars, simply because it is not catalogue policy to list a relatively common mint stamp for less than its used counterpart. For every collector who seeks it in used condition there may be a hundred who seek it mint, and the catalogue is written to reflect the more popular demand. Were it otherwise, it would be conceivable that some enterprising souls might take the mint block and render it much more valuable simply by placing on it a postmark similar to the one of the period in which it was used.

Thus it can readily be seen that availability of material is a concomitant of value, since availability creates demand. Collectors by and large being a group of individuals who will be more interested in buying what is readily available, the number who feel that the pleasure of the chase is at least equal to the pride of possession is limited indeed.

To return to used blocks, one can easily build up an enviable collection of these of the past forty years or so. The great popularity of stamp collecting since about 1920 has assured an extensive backlog of material, in this case used blocks. Many mint blocks were intentionally used on mail matter, simply to make them available. But before this era, what used blocks presently exist came about by mere chance. Mail users and postal clerks in earlier days preferred to use a single twenty-cent stamp on mail matter rather than a block of four of the five-cent value. It was more convenient, certainly, to use a single dollar stamp rather than two blocks, one of the twelve-cent denomination and one of the thirteen-cent, which would have achieved the same purpose.

There are a large number of collectors of used blocks, and it is no difficult matter to assemble a complete collection of used blocks from approximately 1920 to date. But the difficulty of extending the collection to 1910 is a considerable one, and if one seeks to go back even to the turn of the century, he is treading a path that few before him have successfully done. The popularity of the material cannot be gainsaid, nor can the demand for it be minimized. The lack of availability simply limits the number who provide the demand. Admittedly scarce these items are, but because of the far greater and more insistent demand, the mint counterparts will invariably bring a higher price.

Earlier we mentioned that in the field of United States stamps there are any number that are so rare that a period of ten years or more might elapse before one comes on the market. The unpopularity of some of these can easily explain the nominal price at which they sell. There is a very limited demand for a stamp surcharged SPECIMEN, for example. On some sheets of these one stamp had the surcharge misspelled SEPCIMEN; on a few, since only one sheet of the surcharged variety was issued, the

SEPCIMEN error that one encounters becomes a unique stamp, fully as rare as the aforementioned British Guiana one-cent of 1851. The price does not reflect the fact.

But there are United States postage stamps of great rarity, spaces for which are provided in every album, that sell at prices far less than common sense might dictate. A five-cent orange-brown stamp issued in 1875, Scott #42, was issued in a total of 878 copies. Perhaps half the original supply is available to collectors today; the stamp catalogues for $65.00. The one-cent stamp of the same series comes with a listed variety, a cracked plate, of which 91 examples at the very most can possibly exist; it is not even priced in the catalogue, but specimens in all probability would not bring more than $75.00 or $100. There is no question of their rarity; certainly there is a good demand for it; the factor of popularity, however, is missing, and the demand for it is therefore considerably reduced from what it would be were it a commemorative stamp, for example, or an air mail.

Status being a popular word these days, often a stamp that might otherwise be in relatively little demand achieves a measure of desirability when its previous owner was someone of note. This has been seen in the case of the Roosevelt collection, where otherwise common (and easily obtainable) stamps were run up to fantastic levels simply because they had been owned by a president of the United States. The ability to say that a certain stamp had previously been owned by a Ferrari, by a Hind, or by a Casparry gives that particular stamp a distinction over and beyond what might otherwise be the case.

This fact is well known. How else can one account for the tremendous crowds and the tremendous prices when a fabulous collection comes on the market? It cannot be questioned that in many collections being built today there are exceptional stamps that are the equal in every way of their counterparts in the "name" collections. Earlier we mentioned the twenty-four-cent purple stamp, offered in the Ernest R. Jacobs collection, which brought a tremendous price, despite a defect. Who can deny that were the same stamp offered for sale in a collection assembled by an unknown collector, the price realized would have been far, far less?

Yet these are market facts that must be reckoned with. The Jacobs stamp is now "pedigreed." The distinction it has achieved because of its previous esteemed ownership will probably always endow it with a status that will assure a liberal price whenever it comes up for sale, at least as long as the Jacobs name is known and respected. But let it someday find itself in the hands of an owner to whom the Jacobs name has no magic, and the value of the stamp will drop to a more nominal figure—unless, of course, another collector with the reputation, the knowledge, and the keen sense of condition that Jacobs possessed recognizes it for what it is.

Just as there are many buyers who set great store on status, and will buy only in auctions that offer the possessions of the greats of philately, so there are many who completely ignore the "name" sales, and with full confidence in their own ability to judge price, condition, and resalability, will give most of their attention to collections of figures who are less known. These stamps may be in every way the equal of the pedigreed ones, which sell for immeasurably more. Many of tomorrow's name collections are being built up in this manner. We leave it to the judgment of the individual buyer as to which is the better procedure to follow.

Here again knowledge plays a great part. There truly is no substitute for knowledge. Things have been learned about certain stamps in recent years that were unknown earlier. Research taking place today will affect the prices of stamps to be sold in the future. It is known for certain that our first issue of postage stamps, the 1847 series, was put on sale July 1, 1847. Contemporary newspaper accounts confirm the fact so definitely that the statement cannot be questioned. Yet the earliest known example ever found is postmarked more than a week later. A fortune awaits the finder of one postmarked July 1, 1847, and a substantial financial reward will come the way of someone who can even beat the presently known date. When it is found, it will be only partly luck; much of the reward will be owing to knowledge of the fact that this is something to be sought.

Our next series, that of 1851, also appeared on July 1, but on this item several letters bearing the three-cent, the most common of the series, are known. They command prices up to several hundred dollars. Is it luck or knowledge that has resulted in one collector's finding no less than three of these in a five-year period?

The ramifications of philately are scarcely understood, even by the veteran philatelist. Almost daily we learn of a field of philately from which someone finds intense pleasure. Although first-day-cover collecting is engaged in by hundreds of thousands of collectors, we once encountered a collector who collects first-night covers. We thought he was joking when he mentioned the fact. He shunned the conventional cacheted professionally made first-day cover, with the inevitable postmark showing the time as 9 A.M. or 10 A.M. Instead, he scrounged through the wastebaskets in post offices, in his office, and among the rubbish in his apartment house, seeking covers used in other than philatelic mail, bearing a new stamp, with the first-day postmark, but bearing a time indication during the afternoon or evening of the same day. Such a collection must be profoundly rare; in fact, I doubt if there is another, but the owner was fully aware of its lack of value, since he was collecting primarily for the pleasure.

Of the countless byways of philately, some of them engaged in by vast numbers of collectors, are such widely-followed fields as meters, precancels, state tax revenues, airport dedication covers, topical stamps, flight covers, Christmas seals, and baggage labels. We have seen interesting collections of all these fields. We have had adherents of these various specialties expound on them with such fervor and such enthusiasm that the extreme pleasure and the intense devotion which their pet field engendered were truly wonderful things to behold. It should not be the case that the dollar sign is paramount in the building of any sort of collection, and it is highly desirable that the rewards of any hobby should be greatest in pleasure and satisfaction. Nevertheless, we must assume that the reader of this book is interested in knowing the facts, and in seeing that his hobby dollar is spent in such manner that it will assure the greatest return when the day comes when he wishes to sell.

The fact is unfortunately true that pleasant as the collecting of meters and precancels, baggage labels, and Christmas seals may be, most people who collect them do so merely because they understandably want to share in the pleasures of collecting, without being obliged to spend the money that collecting conventional stamps entails. We certainly do not want to discredit them when we say this. We have seen a precancel collector show a greater knowledge of his subject than many a collector who has put together an enviable collection of plate number blocks; the amount of money spent certainly is no barometer of the caliber of the philatelist.

Of course there are exceptions. We know a collection of Christmas seals built up by a collector in Fitchburg, Massachusetts, who has spared no expense in obtaining the rarest and most valuable items in his field. We know a doctor in the Midwest who would travel across the country to obtain one of the very few precancels presently missing from his collection. But we are not referring to these. We refer simply to the greater number of collectors in these allied fields of philately, all of them fine people, who find that for one reason or another they simply cannot or do not want to compete with the more conventional type of collector.

If the side-line collector realizes this, he has no disappointment ahead of him. But let the side-line collector build up his collection carefully, no matter how well he mounts it, no matter how thoroughly he studies it, no matter how skillful the presentation, when the day comes that he wants to sell it he has a rude shock ahead of him. Whether he wants to admit it or not, his potential market is his confreres, the very people who are in the same field simply because they cannot or do not want to spend appreciable sums on their hobby.

For the fact is that in a world geared to a system that is based on money the hope of financial reward can come only with an expenditure of some sort, be it labor, experience, or the investment of capital itself. The man who puts out money for stamps, according to the degree of acumen and good fortune he has, will find that he can get money for them when he sells. Whether it is more than he paid, or less, depends on many considerations. But the man who boasts that his collection has cost him nothing should not be surprised if, when he tries to sell it, his prospects seem to share his original ideas about what his collection is worth.

Every collector in daily life meets many people who greet news of his philatelic interest with enthusiasm. "Why, I have a neighbor" (or here one can read "brother," "father," "uncle," "grandfather," or "boss") "who collects, and he has a truly magnificent collection." Come to think of it, in some forty-five years, since our own philatelic interests became well rooted, we have met thousands of persons who have either collected, or who knew of someone who did, but in all that time we have never heard of anyone who did not have a "fabulous" or a "magnificent" collection.

If one asks these people a simple but revealing question, such as, "Where does he buy his stamps?" the answer is almost always the same. "Oh, he doesn't buy stamps, he gets them in other ways." In the eyes of the nonphilatelist, simply buying stamps is one of the more reprehensible ways to collect. The inference is that anyone can do that. No, Uncle Jerome exercises far greater ingenuity in building up his magnificent collection. Uncle Jerome's nephew may not know where his uncle obtains his stamps, but he is certain they didn't come from dealers.

The answer is, of course, the tipoff as to the true status of the magnificent collection, for in all our years in philately we have yet to come across a valuable collection that did not cost someone a pretty pile of money. Of course one can be lucky enough to find a fine collection in his attic, or to pick it up for a song in an auction of personal effects where no one recognized it for what it was other than the buyer. But even in such an unlikely event the facts are that someone somewhere along the line paid a fair sum for the contents. Valuable items, be they stamps, diamonds, real estate, or Cadillac cars, just don't grow on trees, free for the picking, or lie unappreciated in wastebaskets, free for the taking.

We have not yet mentioned the vast number of people who have a brother, father, uncle, grandfather, or boss who possesses fabulous and magnificent collections of complete United States sheets. "It's a tremendous collection," they will say. "He even has it in special albums that he pays $10.00 each for, and he keeps it in a safe-deposit vault, and it is insured for $50,000" (or $100,000 or $250,000, according to the individual's reluctance to exaggerate).

It has happened to all of us, and it will happen many times again. The old adage "what you get for nothing is generally worth nothing" holds as true for stamps as it does for most other things. A stamp collection of value simply cannot be built up without an investment of good solid cash, unless one is fortunate enough to find a means by which he can obtain at little or no cost stamps that the original owners, through ignorance or design, find that they would rather give away than sell.

And that meter picked up in the post-office basket with an inverted year date, or which reads "1691" instead of "1961" may be extremely rare, even if it cost the fortunate finder nothing. And the precancel with the city name upside down may occupy a place of distinction on the album page, as does the double-printed imperforate Christmas seal, or the baggage label printed sideways, but while one cannot doubt their rarity, the factor of value does not necessarily accompany.

For in philately rarity does not necessarily make for value.

8. *Cash in on fads, don't become a victim of them.*

In a poker game there is a certain amount of money to be won. It equals exactly the total amount of money that those playing put into the game. Some of them may have additional funds in their pockets while they play, but as long as those funds are uncommitted, they cannot be won or lost as long as the game remains on a cash basis.

In other words, what is to be won by the fortunate ones must come from the pockets of the less fortunate.

The philatelic poker game is much kinder to the players. In philately, under certain circumstances, all those participating may emerge winners. There are few other fields of endeavor where both buyer and seller can congratulate themselves on a purchase or a sale, and each actually has just cause for congratulations.

Philately has as one of its charms the possibility of the very same item being sold time and again, each time at a higher price, with each successive owner obtaining for it more than he paid for it.

Dealers particularly find this to their liking. It is by no means uncommon for Dealer X to sell a certain stamp to Buyer A, of course at a profit to himself, only to sell it for Mr. A's estate at a later date, at a tidy profit for the latter, to the buyer, Mr. B., who will probably someday sell it back to Dealer X at a profit to himself. Even the undertaking business, which is held up by so many as the ideal profession since sooner or later everyone becomes a customer, cannot hold a candle to philately. Seldom if ever does an undertaker serve the same client twice.

Observers of human frailties may comment, as they usually do, on the enslavement of the species by those who set the fashion trend. Dior, Givenchy, and Balenciaga are less interested in making the female form attractive than in inducing Milady to cast aside her fine raiment of yesterday in favor of what is to be worn today, and again to be cast off tomorrow.

The philatelist sometimes finds himself similarly enslaved by fashion, although he is more the victim of his own plight than Milady. Milady wouldn't think of venturing out with a hemline two inches higher than the one decreed for that season; there is no one who tells the philatelist that he must conform. But too often conform he must.

We have no fault to find with the monotonous sameness of most collections, especially if they bring pleasure to the possessor. A dealer finds it a bit tedious to have to admire a collection a client brings in for view, and sometimes the dealer finds it difficult to breathe a measure of sincerity into his oh's and ah's when he sees a printed page with a mint single of each stamp in precisely the same arrangement that the album publisher decreed.

The collector who uses a blank album is in a somewhat more enviable position, for he can at least vary the page arrangement to suit his own aesthetic desires. The customary arrangement in this case is a mint single, a used single, a mint block, and a mint plate number block, and if the page is large enough, a first-day cover thrown in.

One can find little fault or criticism with the conventional arrangement mentioned, for such a collection when offered for sale generally finds a ready market, and, as has been emphasized, it is the ultimate salability of the collection that concerns the reader of this book.

On the fringe of conventional collecting one finds the true fads. There is no limit to the fields which these may encompass. Fads come and go. Some may last months or years; some may never die, but all share one thing in common: the period during which they are in demand, and thus salable, is limited.

Back in the early 1930s some enterprising individual recalled that his home town was about to celebrate the hundredth anniversary of the installation of the first overhead gas street light, hung from a pole rather than from the eaves of a building. The incident is admittedly fictional but the ingenious chap felt that the anniversary should be celebrated philatelically. He had a rubber stamp made, which pictured his conception of what the gas lamp looked like, and affixing a stamp, he had it postmarked from the local post office at the time and date that the ceremonies attendant to the great improvement were made, but one hundred years later. The collecting of cacheted covers had begun.

Within months collectors all over the country were commemorating events ranging from the hundredth anniversary of the invention of the doughnut to the sixty-third anniversary of the construction of the first indoor privy in Boone, Iowa. Stamp magazines stimulated the demand by listing forthcoming cachets, and collectors stayed up nights preparing covers to be sent to the cachet sponsors. Chambers of commerce soon got in on the act; what better way to get national publicity for Tucumcari, New Mexico, than to let thousands of collectors from one end of the country to the other know that were it not for some inventive genius in Tucumcari, oven doors might have continued to be made of steel rather than have a glass door through which the roast beef might be observed while it was cooking.

Cachet sponsors found that they could pick up a certain

amount of loose change by making a nominal charge for their effusions, and with the stamp magazines giving them free publicity, and the customer paying the postage both ways, a built-in profit without any attendant expense was assured. Magazines countered by refusing to list cachets for which more than ten cents per cover "handling charge" was asked.

One still encounters bundles of these cacheted covers. In fact, one of the principal sources today for used commemoratives of that period is these very covers. Tens of thousands of them have been bought by dealers at nominal prices, sometimes even less than the original face value of the stamps. The stamps, when soaked off, can pay a very tidy profit. In this case it is not the original collector who succumbed to the fad who found it profitable; it is the one who profited by his actions, sometimes many years later.

The writer got in on the act on two occasions. In 1934 the fifth anniversary of the stock-market crash took place, and the writer was then employed in Wall Street. A cachet consisting of a bit of the ticker tape that went through the ticker during the very hour in which the debacle had occurred five years earlier was arranged. A multigraph machine in the office where we were employed supplied the necessary wording, and an obliging clerk at the Wall Street branch of the New York Post Office arranged to postmark the envelopes at 3 P.M., the time at which the stock market closed the day of the crash. No less than 1,400 collectors scrambled to obtain specimens of this rare philatelic item; at ten cents per cover, the venture returned a tidy $14.00 profit. Envelopes and stamps were supplied by the recipients, and the labor involved in their preparation was a labor of love. This was philately in the richest sense we then felt.

The next year the streetcar line traversing Madison Avenue celebrated its hundredth anniversary. It was the first streetcar line in the United States. The success of the stock-market crash venture encouraged the writer to produce a second cachet, and this time a modest investment of $2.00 converted a sketch of a horse-drawn trolley car, turned out by an artistically inclined fellow office worker, into a rubber-stamp cachet. The philatelic monstrosity thus created returned a profit even larger than the stock-market-crash cover.

Occasionally these very covers come to us from various sources. Sometimes dealers come upon them in the purchase of a collection and accumulation, and hasten to remind us of our philatelic infancy. Pleasure each original owner must have had from the possession, but it is doubtful whether anyone ever found his dime well spent, unless perchance he used on the envelope a commemorative stamp which today has a much greater value.

As air-mail routes spread over the face of the nation, the smallest towns found that to be modern an airport must be created. Many simply chased the cows off the nearest patch of flat ground, erected a sign and a wind sock, and announced themselves possessed of an airport. Stamp collectors helped the deception along by posting covers at the nearest post office at the time and date of the opening of the airport; the once-popular field of airport-dedication covers had been created.

Lindbergh's solo flight to Paris was followed by innumerable cacheted covers every time Lindbergh paid a visit to a town which had had nothing memorable happen to it since the school burned down many years before. When public sentiment thought that Lindbergh should once again fly the route out of Springfield, Illinois, that he had flown in his pre-Paris flight days, so many stamp collectors forwarded covers to Springfield to accompany him on the flight that when he took off he was followed by four additional planes, piloted by other fliers carrying the load. These covers, bearing the hand-stamped cachet "LINDBERGH AGAIN CARRIES THE MAIL," turn up with such frequency that today, recalling the comparatively small space available for mailbags in those pioneer flying crates, one wonders how even five planes could have originally carried them. Such covers are of nominal value today, for they invariably carry a Lindbergh air-mail stamp, which sells on the current market for about forty cents. Although thousands have been soaked off for the stamp, the supply of flown covers seemingly is inexhaustible.

Many collectors lose sight of the fact that the stamp is the basic thing to collect. There are many things that can be done with a stamp, but philately basically is the collecting of stamps. Stamp collectors we will always have with us. A stamp mounted in a collection will always have some value; a block of stamps will always be in demand. But changing the identity of the stamp and making it only an incidental part of something else to collect are giving in to the temptation to make it part and parcel of a fad which can have little to recommend it, insofar as philatelic value is concerned.

Collectors have cut stamps in half, diagonally, vertically, and horizontally, and succeeded in convincing a postal clerk who was more gullible than intelligent that half of a four-cent stamp is as good as a two-cent stamp, and should be honored as such. The fact that in the early days of the West, when a six-cent stamp did not exist, post offices tolerated the use of half of a twelve-cent stamp to pay such a rate, seemed to give philatelic respectability to the act. Such modern freaks are valueless.

Probably the most widely followed fad of modern times is the collecting of first-day covers. On some commemorative stamps in recent years as many as a million covers have been prepared and sent. It is today such big business that dozens of dealers find it a profitable business, and they are able to make satisfactory livings catering to the demand. The Post Office itself encourages the collecting of first-day covers, as well it should. A mint stamp sold to a collector may at some later date be put on an envelope, and the Post Office will have to give postal service to it. The stamp used on a first-day cover has lost its postal value forever.

We have seen some fine collections of first-day covers in our time. The artistic eye, in appraising a collection of any kind, is always attracted by uniformity. The collector of stamps tries to obtain that goal by arranging the stamps symmetrically on the page. The collector of first-day covers achieves it with a uniformity of cachet on envelopes of the same size.

First-day covers have been with us for more than a century; quite a few are known of the three-cent 1851, including at least one wherein the sender of the letter was aware of the novelty of the new stamp. Cachets as we know them today are a recent development.

In the late 1920s some collectors prepared plain rubber-stamped cachets, sometimes illustrated, calling attention to the new stamp. In 1932, with the Washington Bicentennial issue, the Post Office obligingly supplied a hand-stamped cachet picturing Washington's home at Mount Vernon. By the time the Arbor Day and the Olympic stamps appeared in 1932, envelopes with brightly-colored printed cachets were the rule.

Dignified, engraved cachets on fine envelope stock came some years later, about 1940, with the Famous Americans.

A lot of fun has been poked at first-day-cover collecting. Some of it has been justified. It is ridiculous on the face of it for a neatly addressed cover to be turned down, simply because it has been addressed. If a cover is supposed to have gone through the mail, how could it have done so without an address?

The date itself on a first-day cover means little. For a month ahead of time covers are being postmarked with the date that collectors set such store by; a month after that date an obliging post office will still run one through for you if you complain that your original cover did not get a legible postmark.

A collection of anything in philately, intelligently assembled and designed to express the theme desired, is not an object of derision. But we think we do know why most collectors who admit to collecting first-day covers find their admission is greeted with laughter.

The juvenile collector likes first-day covers because he gets more for his dime in that field than in any other: a large envelope, a gaudy picture, a pictorial postmark. Two of them will fill a page. Where else in philately can you get a bargain like that?

The somewhat advanced collector likes first-day covers because for the price of the envelopes and postage he can get ten identical items that he is certain will go "up." Then when and if they do he not only gets his own for nothing, but will have nine others to sell at a profit.

The only difficulty is that the very people to whom he wishes to sell his nine covers have nine covers of their own to sell him.

If one collects first-day covers for pleasure, that is, we're all for it. In our thirty years in philately we have met one or two who told us that that was their goal, and we admired them for it. But against this we have met hundreds, yea, thousands, who collect these as an "investment."

Just where the "investment" is in taking a mint four-cent stamp, always worth four cents in postage on a letter, and getting it canceled, thus reducing its value to that of a used stamp, we'll never know.

One of the biggest dealers in first-day covers was a fine old gentleman, E. P. Haworth, of Kansas City. We knew Mr. Haworth well. At a stamp show in St. Louis, about fifteen years ago, we had adjoining booths. We asked Mr. Haworth how he could reconcile his extensive advertising along the theme "Buy First-Day Covers as an Investment" with the undeniable fact that collections of them were almost impossible to sell.

Mr. Haworth pointed to the Walloons, the Norse, and other stamps of the period, explaining how much they were worth on first-day covers in relation to face value. We tried to explain that it is the value of the stamp in used condition that determines the value of the first-day cover; we explained that the greatest source of used singles of the scarcer commemoratives of that period was first-day and first-flight covers.

Mr. Haworth died not long ago, and his tremendous stock of first-day covers came on the market. The stock was widely offered but few expressed an interest. Then it was finally sold, but the statistics of the sale should interest those who are still amassing quantities of recent first-day covers with the idea of selling them at a fabulous profit.

The Haworth stock consisted of between 250,000 and 300,000 covers. (It is interesting to note that the dealer who finally purchased the lot didn't consider them valuable enough to waste the time to count them.) They started with the Flag issue, and they ran to 1957. All had cachets, all were unaddressed. By the rules of first-day-cover collecting they should have been prime material, easily sold. The face value (this the dealer counted) was $20,500.00.

We won't mention the actual price at which the lot was finally sold, except to say that it was a fraction of the original face value. If the stamps had been retained mint, at least the discount which they would bring would have been minimal. The countless hours of work placing them on envelopes, the cost of the more than two hundred thousand envelopes, even without the printing; the task of moving 3,000 pounds of covers from Kansas City to New York, this was an investment?

It is much more difficult to anticipate a future fad than to pay tribute to a going one.

When back in 1917 the two-cent stamp of that era turned out to have a few five-cent stamps in the same sheet, a very few foresighted collectors conceived the idea of putting the mint errors on envelopes, and getting them postmarked. To many it may have seemed a foolish thing to do, but with literally thousands of them existing mint, the act was not quite so foolhardy as it might seem. A number of these covers have come down to us today. If one wonders as to the relative value of a five-cent error in mint condition as compared to one used on a cover of the period, he has but to look in the catalogue and see which is the better property. The smart boys were indeed the ones who took a fairly common mint stamp and completely changed its philatelic status by getting it canceled. If a handful of collectors do something of this sort, it can repay handsome dividends; if a million collectors do it, as they do with first-day covers, the result is an item that is likely to be a drug on the market for as long as there are collectors.

We ourselves took a leaf from this same book when the Defense issue of 1940 began to appear lacking perforations in a vertical direction. The Bureau of Engraving and Printing found that the steel they needed to replace the fast-wearing-out perforation machines was not obtainable. The machines themselves, working overtime to turn out not only postage stamps but defense and savings stamps as well, wore out even faster. All three values of the series, the one-cent, two-cent, and three-cent, appeared in part perforate condition. The writer, as did many other dealers of the time, found his mail flooded with offers of the stamps from fortunate finders. So common were they that for a period one could buy virtually unlimited quantities of them for a dollar per pair. (The vastness of the stamp market and its ability to absorb even tremendous quantities of a popular item are shown by the fact that today, a bit more than two decades later, these list for $30.00 per pair.)

With such quantities available, the writer conceived the idea of using some on covers, just as some farseeing individuals had used the then-common five-cent errors on covers twenty-three years before. A number of such covers were prepared and posted. We have yet to hear of anyone else's having done it. None of them have ever been sold, and the entire lot is still intact. There is no catalogue listing for them, for to our knowledge none has ever appeared on the market. But when and if they are sold, we are certain that the price they will bring will be infinitely more than the same stamps are currently bringing in mint condition.

In Wall Street there is an adage: It doesn't matter if you are a bull or a bear, as long as you aren't a pig. A bear, of course, looks for a drop in the market, and bases his position on that likelihood. A bull expects a rise. But a pig, not satisfied with an adequate profit, holds on, well past the time at which he should have sold, and ends up with nothing.

There is another saying in Wall Street: No one ever went broke taking a profit.

The philatelist seeking to make his hobby pay him a reward can well ponder both of these aphorisms.

In the field of foreign topical issues both adages will apply.

The ability of the stamp collector to put his money into stamps that have been touted to the sky in advertisements, only to see his investment sicken, wither, and die, is a tribute to the statement that hope springs eternal in the human soul.

The one hundred and fiftieth anniversary of the United States Constitution in 1937 was the occasion for the issuance of a large number of sets by many foreign countries, in tribute to this

118

country's contribution to the world. Tens of thousands of sets were sold to tens of thousands of this country's collectors. Foreign countries reaped a tremendous harvest of dollars, and collectors received in exchange a quantity of brightly colored bits of paper. Two years later there was probably nothing in the catalogue more difficult to sell.

In rapid succession foreign countries hastened to commemorate the New York World's Fair of 1939, the death of Roosevelt in 1945, the hundredth anniversary of our first postage stamp in 1947, the Brussels World's Fair of 1958, and the Olympic Games of 1960. One can pick up any stamp magazine of any of those years, and by studying the ads, easily ascertain what the most popular stamps of the particular period were. But what happened when the next issue came along?

This year it is the stamps issued to commemorate the United States of Europe, the EUROPA sets. This was perhaps the greatest debacle of all. While some of the earlier EUROPA stamps of earlier years were genuinely scarce, because of the small numbers issued, those issued more recently were issued under the most vicious chicanery ever surrounding a stamp issue. Sovereign nations, in their greed for the philatelists' dollar, restricted supplies, gave stamps to some who paid bribes to officials, and denied them to others who had been steady patrons for earlier issues. Intentional "errors" were created, and false rumors started to stimulate sales. Once their supplies were disposed of, the price was allowed to collapse. Belated additional supplies suddenly became available on some, thus further contributing to the collapse in price.

At this writing the EUROPA stamps are dead indeed. Those who were stampeded into buying them at the tail end, on the strength of rumor and hysteria as to how scarce they would be, are now nursing their wounds. Their position in years to come will be no better than that of those collectors who paid $19.50 for the set of stamps Nicaragua issued in 1945 portraying President Roosevelt working on his stamps. Today's market value: about $6.00.

The fearful racketeering that has engulfed certain phases of philately is hardly likely to abate. It surely never will as long as collectors continue to pay tribute to individuals and nations which make no bones of the fact that they are out to exploit them. One can hardly blame the dealers who handle these stamps. Most dealers handling the ill-fated EUROPA issues of 1961 and 1962 lost more money on them than they made on the earlier sets, some of which proved to be desirable philatelic property.

Prohibition was a failure in this country because the public insisted on continuing to buy liquor, whatever the difficulty, whatever the cost. Had this demand not been a fact, it would have been economically unprofitable for liquor to be sold. As long as the collector insists on buying issues of those nations which have time and again exploited him, victimized him, cheated him, and swindled him, those same countries will continue to play him for a sucker. And as long as the collector who finds that his dealer refuses to handle these stamps then goes to the next dealer who does, no stamp dealer can afford to refuse to handle them.

The "new look" in stamps for the future involves causes and projects that are of themselves laudable, but which are tied up with the issue of stamps in order to attract money from stamp collectors. Although the Malaria issues of 1962 were not the first, they are but the forerunner of many more good causes that will use philately to rake in the money.

Certainly there is no one who will not do what he can to fight malaria, but many of those who are contributing to the fight against malaria, receiving sets of stamps in exchange, do not realize that but a fraction of their money actually goes to fight malaria. One can only conjecture how much actually finds its way into the research laboratory.

With so many dozens of diseases as yet unconquered, the possibilities for extracting money from well-meaning and philanthropic philatelists is almost unlimited.

Advertisements in magazines, and even on the radio, exhorting readers and listeners to "buy stamps to fight malaria" do give the impression that all money used for purchase of these stamps is used for the battle, when nothing is further from the truth. One cannot but wonder whether there may be some charitable individuals making out checks for the purchase of Malaria issues who feel that in so doing they are making a charitable deduction that will be accepted by the Internal Revenue as a charitable donation.

Some of these issues may turn out "good"; more likely than not, most of them will before many years join the Constitution sets, the Columbus Lighthouse sets, the Brussels World's Fair sets, in the limbo of forgotten and no-longer popular issues. And buyers will point to the one or two sets which they have purchased, and with pride mention the tremendous profit they have in them, at the same time failing to mention the greater number of sets on which they will never see their cost returned. They have indeed helped the fight against malaria, but had they known the real facts, killing a half-dozen mosquitoes might have been a greater contribution!

There are so many legitimate issues to collect, and so many stamps of proven desirability that it is wasted sympathy to feel sorry for those who have succumbed to the lure of the "get-rich-quick" boys who live on the fringe of philately. The "ambassadors" who visit the head of the Dutch philatelic section every six months may not enjoy success with him, but as long as tens of thousands of collectors, mostly in the United States, but abroad as well, continue to absorb their odoriferous issues, so long will they continue to ply their profitable trade.

One can only conjecture as to what would happen if the millions of dollars presently going into the pockets of foreign postal officials and politicians were to be spent for desirable philatelic merchandise, the type of stamp that would be much more likely to pay the collector the reward he feels he is getting when he buys a dozen sets of stamps from a dozen different countries commemorating the Boy Scout anniversary, or the latest brainstorm, the conquest of malaria. But collectors who are willing to think for themselves, collectors who are unwilling to become part of a well-developed and thought-out scheme for separating them from their money and giving them in exchange some stamps which in a few years will be worth much less than they paid for them, are few indeed.

Philatelic fads will always be with us, but if one uses a bit of common sense, he can actually profit from them.

One thing done by many philatelists is to study not the selling ads of various dealers, but their buying ads.

One can more often than not assume that a professional knows what he is doing. If his ads on EUROPA material offer the 1962 issues for sale, but mention that he would like to buy some of the 1957 issues, one can safely assume that the latter will be the more desirable property to own. Here, again, we are advising the collector who seeks to collect profitably, the one who wants to spend his money wisely, and in such manner that when he decides to sell, he will be able to get back the greater part of his original investment, and possibly a good bit more. The suggestion is definitely not for the purely amateur collector who collects EUROPA stamps, who wants them complete, and is comparatively indifferent to the prospects of getting as much, or more, or less for them when he decides to sell.

As a general rule, dealers are pretty straightforward in their ads, whether they are buying or selling. But the ads seeking to buy tell a great deal more about the market than those offering to sell. And when a number of dealers spend their good money to take an advertisement to buy stamps of certain issues, or certain countries, one can be quite certain there is a good reason for it.

In the past year or two the stamp magazines have contained many advertisements of dealers seeking to buy German stamps. Many of their offers were well in excess of the Scott catalogue prices. These offers were not made because of any desire to become philanthropists. They were prompted by the very real fact that economic conditions in Germany had so improved in recent years that the German dealers and collectors were trying to repatriate many of the very stamps that they had exported a few short years ago when they needed foreign money so urgently to build up their economy.

And in the light of the 1962 Scott catalogue, some of their offers did not seem quite so generous as they had a few months previously, for the catalogue, although it may take a year to catch up with the market, since it appears annually, had indeed caught up. What was "over catalogue" in 1961 proved in a number of cases to be "half catalogue" in 1962. Well off, indeed, was the collector who added to his collection those same items sought by dealers while they were still available at a modest price.

The collector who stays in a popular field and seeks stamps only of those popular countries as a general rule is doing a wise thing. By confining his activities to those issues for which there is the greatest demand, he is certain that when his collection comes up for sale it will be offered to the widest possible market. There are many advantages to this.

Correct though this may be, there are certain definite advantages in refusing to follow the beaten path and striking out into untrodden fields. There are many collectors who will vehemently insist that therein lies the most certain road to philatelic profit, and there is a great deal of history to prove them correct.

There is no question but that the buying opportunities in a seldom-collected field are far, far greater than those in one that is popularly followed. If one additionally makes a study of his stamps, and knows what is available, and what he needs, the mere fact that he has few competitors in a less popular field gives him an inestimable advantage in locating what can actually be rare material at very reasonable prices. The dealer with a rare Afghanistan cover will be happy indeed to sell it, even if he knows how rare it is, when he realizes that he knows only one possible buyer for it.

We have seen some wonderful collections made at surprisingly moderate cost by collectors who were determined not to pay tribute to the racketeers who mulct so many collectors with such ease. These are the collectors of such countries as Tibet, Nepal, Colombian States, Russian locals, and Mexican revenues. They are less interested in the ultimate value of their collections than most, preferring the honest pleasures of philately, but in keeping with the ironic aspects of philately, of which there are so many, more often than not, when they do sell, their pioneering efforts have paid them a neat reward.

One can even pay homage to those very issues which we have condemned in these pages by seeking them in legitimate used condition. The chase will be a difficult one, but the rewards will be fully compensatory.

Ernest A. Kehr, author of one of the finest background books on philately, *The Romance of Stamp Collecting,* mentioned one way to "join them, and beat them" in his New York *Herald Tribune* column in 1961. Kehr shows how one may still collect the "made-for-stamp-collectors" pretty labels, without paying tribute to the so-called "philatelic agents" responsible for their distribution.

"Many of 1960s stamps will rise in value; many others will probably be selling for less in years to come. The true collector is unconcerned: he builds his album as a form of recreation, fun, and pleasure, and takes his chances. He charges expenditures to enjoyment in the same spirit that he spends money for theater tickets or a special night out, without expecting a refund after he's had fun.

"Future scarcity can be predicted; future values cannot. Some of the 1960 crop of a record-breaking number of new issues are certain to be rarities a decade (or less) from now. Only a minimum of careful observation is necessary to name them all.

"During 1960 the philatelic market has seen the establishment of numerous new postal administrations, some of which have adopted policies of producing far more stamps than are postally necessary. Some, moreover, have engaged professional merchandisers to promote sales through saturation advertising and publicity.

"Such issues—as unused specimens, or on specially prepared 'first-day covers'—because they have been placed directly in the philatelic market, will be available for generations to come. Relatively few of the tens of thousands printed will be 'lost' since they were not widely used by natives of the lands producing them.

"The collector, then, who obtains—if he can—any of these 'promoted' issues on legitimately used mail will have real rarities of tomorrow.

"This is especially true of countries whose normal annual mail poundage is particularly small because of the illiteracy of their natives, or the lack of foreign trade. Even the low-values of ordinary stamp sets from such places as Bhutan, Nepal, Maldives, Mauritania, Guinea, Norfolk, Papua or Yemen, for instance, legitimately used on mail are exceedingly scarce. Specially made 'commemoratives' and the unnecessarily high denominations are all but non-existent in such used condition. These, then, will be the 'great rarities' for which philatelists will be hunting (and probably paying good prices) from now on.

"One good word of advice. When and if a collector finds such stamps on regularly delivered mail addressed to an individual or business firm, they should be left on the full original envelope to show that they actually did postal service and were not simply prepared for sale to a collector."

It will be no easy task, finding stamps of some of these newer nations in postally used condition, but it can be done. Their consulates and embassies may be contacted; religious organizations that send them missionaries may be of help; import and export houses that deal with them commercially may have material to offer. As a last resort, one may always start a correspondence with a philatelist in the country itself; if none is known, the United States embassy there will generally be able to find someone willing and happy to correspond.

There is no question but that writing a check and mailing it to your dealer for a new set of Mali stamps picturing the ring-necked frontback is the easiest way to get them, but the philatelic rewards in having the entire set postally used, and at little or no cost, is one that few enough philatelists appreciate.

Philatelic fads will always be with us, and many branches of collecting now engaging the attention of collectors will die by the wayside, to be followed by others as yet unthought of. All of them will be designed to bring pleasure and satisfaction to their adherents. The fortunate ones will be those who have their pleasure and satisfaction and at the same time find that it pays to cash in on fads and not become a victim of them.

9. *Don't be a slave to the catalogue.* We have recommended careful study of the advertisements of dealers in the weekly magazines. They will tell far more about the current market than any printed catalogue or price list. What is more, they will contain the latest, most recent information, almost as up to date as today's newspaper.

You may see two advertisements next to each other. In one a dealer is offering to pay full Scott value for a set of Vatican air-mail stamps. You may be sure that the dealer is not spending his money merely to impress readers with his generosity. He possesses knowledge that the prices of these Vatican air-mail stamps in the current catalogue are too low. Perhaps he already knows that in Italy dealers are paying far more than our own catalogue price for them. Sometimes it takes a year or two for our catalogue to catch up with the market, especially when a sudden boom takes place in the stamps' country of origin.

Adjacent to the advertisement mentioned above is one offering to sell Vatican stamps. Such an advertisement appeared not long ago in one of our magazines, inserted by Jack Nalbandian, a Rhode Island dealer. Taking advantage of the extreme popularity of the stamps of the Vatican, he offered Scott #127, the 17 lira 1949, a stamp listing in Scott at $1.50 each. His price was $7.50 per hundred, with a further reduction to $68.50 if a thousand copies were purchased. This latter price

128

works out to almost one-twenty-fifth of the Scott catalogue price.

Collectors who do not understand the difficulties of producing a catalogue that is always right on the mark will gather from these extremes that the catalogue is useless as a means of determining the market. Surely it would seem to be so when in the same edition, in the same country, one dealer offers to pay full catalogue for certain stamps, while another offers them for sale at one-twentieth of catalogue.

There are approximately one hundred and twenty-five thousand different stamps listed in the Scott catalogue. Most of these are priced in two categories, used and unused. With more than a quarter of a million individual listings, accuracy on every one is impossible. If the proper market price on even 90 per cent of those listed is attained, it is a good record.

But the catalogue appears but once a year. And the press work on the catalogue appearing in October or November was actually completed the previous June or July. Thus one can find it necessary to use a catalogue that not only may have appeared ten or eleven months earlier, but which actually went to press almost a year and a half before. And no catalogue can anticipate prices even a few months ahead, much less a year and a half.

Miner Stamp Company, of Wilkes-Barre, Pennsylvania, in December 1961 offered a quantity of George VI sets of Burma at a twentieth of catalogue. There were 200 sets, each one cataloguing $30.85, and the offered price was $1.49 each.

William Hornadge, a dealer of Dubbo, N.S.W., Australia (Seven Seas Stamp Company), made what would seem to be an even more attractive offer. He offered for sale 20,000 copies of the 21.35 value of the 1954 Romania Workers set, a stamp listed in the Stanley Gibbons catalogue for four shillings each (fifty-six cents). The entire holding catalogued at £5,000 ($14,000); Hornadge offered the lot for sale for £50 ($140), a price that was just one hundredth of catalogue. There was an understandable note of bitterness in the Australian's advertisement:

If you are one of those dyed-in-the-wool collectors who regard Scott or Stanley Gibbons as your Bible on prices, here is your chance to back your judgment with some hard cash. Put up your money, or quit beefing when occasionally a dealer charges over catalogue value for a stamp.

Where does this leave the collector?

It certainly proves that, useful as the catalogue may be, the buyer who places all his faith in it, without supplementing it with additional knowledge, is going to find himself overpaying for a lot of things that would seem to be bargains, and worse yet, getting little of real value simply because the prices seem too high.

The fact is that there are times when a stamp at double catalogue may be a prize bargain, and another stamp—perhaps another stamp in the same set—may be badly overpriced at one tenth of catalogue. The trick is to be able to recognize which is the bargain and which is not. It is one of the functions of this book to point the way. The buying and selling advertisements of reputable dealers in our magazines supply the key.

The stamp business has undergone a tremendous change in the past half century. Collectors themselves have changed in that time.

When the writer was a boy, stamp collecting was one of many hobbies that occupied a growing boy's time. In spring it was baseball, with marbles, mumblety-peg, and swimming taking over as the weather grew warmer. Stamp collecting was one of the more popular cold-weather hobbies, along with chemistry sets, Erector sets, and the making of lead soldiers.

There were adults collecting stamps then, but seldom did

130

they admit to the fact other than to their family and perhaps their closest friends. Parents encouraged their youngsters to collect, knowing that in philately the children were taking a sweet pill that under its sugar coating of pleasure was teaching history, economics, sociology, geography, and, most important of all, a knowledge and awareness of the world about them.

But a king made stamp collecting respectable for adults. King George V was proud to exhibit his collection in his own country and abroad. In 1926 New York put on the greatest philatelic exhibition the world had ever seen, and names that were great in public esteem, politically and industrially, were represented. A governor of New York, soon to be elected president of the United States, unabashedly stated one day, "I owe my life to my hobbies, especially stamp collecting."

Daily papers that had heretofore regarded stamp collecting only as a target for their lampoons, started stamp columns. The Post Office Department in Washington opened up its Philatelic Agency, in order to make it easier for the nation's collectors to buy their stamps at face value without having to visit a dealer. (In a few years the total business done at the Philatelic Agency increased from a few hundred thousand dollars annually to millions.)

Behind this gradual awakening of a hobby giant was a new concept: stamp collecting was being more and more regarded as an investment, and only incidentally as a hobby.

When Junior spent a quarter for a set of Zululand stamps, neither he nor his parents were concerned whether someday he might get back ten cents or fifty cents for the set. When some years later Junior (now called Jack) joined a stamp club, and swapped that set of Zululand (now cataloguing sixty-five cents) for a set of United States Pilgrim stamps, also cataloguing at sixty-five cents, both parties to the transaction were satisfied. The stamp magazines of the time were not advertising specific items for sale. The dealers were not running advertisements seeking to buy certain stamps. The ads themselves had a monotonous sameness about them, so much so that one today wonders just what incentive there may have been for a collector to answer one ad and not another. "We sell at one-third of Scott," one ad would read. "Want lists filled at Scott prices less 66 per cent," read another; a third would read, "Buy from our approvals at one-third of Scott."

United States and British, used and unused, popular and unpopular, all sold on a basis of Scott catalogue, sometimes a third, sometimes a fourth, occasionally at half. The number of what would today be called "advanced collectors" was limited; a handful of dealers made a satisfactory living catering to them. By far the greater number of dealers were content to plod their merry way selling almost every stamp they owned at a predetermined discount from catalogue, at the same time replacing stock by buying collections at a greater discount. (It may be pointed out that there is even today a hardy breed of dealer still pursuing this same policy, although increased costs and collector awareness that catalogue price is not always a criterion, are contributing to the demise of the breed.)

As collecting became more and more respectable for the adult collector, the informed buyers became more concerned as to what they were getting for their money. While Junior might care little that a certain Zululand stamp was obtainable only at full catalogue, his father would try to find out why such was the case. If after visiting three or four dealers he found a uniformity of opinion on the price, he would buy it. He had thus reached the stage where he no longer believed that every stamp in the catalogue was worth one-third of Scott.

As a knowledge of market prices supplanted blind allegiance to catalogue prices, the once-popular method of exchanging stamps between collectors, catalogue value for catalogue value, fell into the discard. Stamp clubs that had been busy hives of activity with collectors exchanging their duplicates found that they had to think of other attractions than this to maintain interest. More and more club members commenced talking dollars and cents in adding to their collections, and less and less about catalogue values.

The trend continues. Today the dollar sign is the all-powerful factor in collecting. It has been years since any dealer offered to fill want lists at a specified discount from catalogue, although a few smaller approval dealers still make the offer in the tiny classified advertisements in our magazines, catering mostly to the beginner collector, who has not yet found out that a stamp at a fifth of catalogue may be a bargain or it may not be.

Old ideas die hard. We still have a good many collectors who place full confidence in the catalogue, without recognizing the fact that many things enter into a stamp's desirability and salability besides the catalogue price.

Which is scarcer, a superb mint three-cent Columbian or a superb mint ten-cent Bell of the Famous Americans (Scott #893)? The Scott pricing gives the answer, someone may say. The former is $3.25, while the latter is $4.25. The scarcity of the ten-cent Bell would seem to be established, since it sells for by far the higher price. But, someone might say, which one is actually the scarcer, in point of numbers issued? The three-cent Columbian was issued in a quantity of 11,501,250 stamps, the ten-cent Bell is but one of 13,726,580 stamps. Which of the two under those circumstances would appear to be the scarcer stamp?

At this point the situation is far from clear. Tens of thousands of collectors purchased the ten-cent Bell when it appeared in 1940, even if additional tens of thousands because of circumstances beyond their control were not able to. Although it is an elusive stamp, it is far from rare. There is scarcely a dealer in the country who handles United States stamps who does not have a few; one could find several thousand copies along New York's Nassau Street without much difficulty if one were simply willing to pay the price.

It is a bit different with the three-cent Columbian. A superb mint example is found but rarely, simply because back in 1893 the stamp printers cared not at all about the stamps they were issuing. A stamp was made to frank a letter, and that was that. In 1940, on the other hand, the Bureau of Printing and Engraving had installed at no little cost a photoelectric eye system on its premises so that stamps intended primarily for philatelic consumption would be produced in much better centering than those stamps intended for ordinary postal use.

How is it that a stamp that is more common from the standpoint of numbers issued can actually be priced higher than another? How is it that a stamp obtainable at cost, which exists in large quantity, should be more valuable than one that not one dealer in five can produce in perfect condition?

There are two answers to this poser: popularity and condition.

There are far more collectors adding the stamps of the past quarter century to their collections than collectors seeking our earliest commemoratives. The average beginning collector starts with the most recent emissions. As time, finances, and desires permit, he progresses backward, year by year. He finds some of the more expensive stamps of recent vintage, such as the ten-cent Bell, a stumbling block, but it is surmounted. But there are so many not quite so easily surmounted stumbling blocks before he finds his way back to 1893, when the Columbians appeared, that he often never reaches that year.

Condition-wise, the cards are stacked against the three-cent Columbian as well. Perhaps 85 per cent of all the ten-cent Bells in existence are reasonably well centered; the electric eye used in their manufacture saw to that. If even 10 per cent of the three-cent Columbians in mint condition are equally well centered, we would suggest that it is a higher figure than experience has shown. If one were to pay full catalogue for a ten-cent Bell, which, incidentally, is almost double the present retail price, would this be a more or a less desirable purchase than an equally perfect three-cent Columbian, at $6.50, or *double* the Scott price?

Inasmuch as the Scott price refers to a stamp in reasonably fine condition or, more exactly, in the condition in which it is ordinarily found, free of defects, the prices of both three-cent Columbian and ten-cent Bell are not out of line. If one compares the latter in the condition in which it is most often found, with the former in the condition in which it is most often found, the prices, far from being incongruous, seem to agree pretty well.

Collectors may have wondered why it is that occasionally a high value of the Columbian or Omaha series will sell at auction for double catalogue, or even more, when such an event never happens to a stamp of which they happen to own a perfect specimen, perhaps even the aforesaid ten-cent Bell. We hope that our account of the reason has made it clear to them.

If collectors would ever make up their minds that the stamps that they should buy first are not the most recent ones, but the stamps that are already scarce (and daily becoming scarcer), they will have taken a long step toward spending their money wisely and building up a collection of substantial value in a much shorter time. For it is simple economics that when a stamp worth a dime doubles in price one has made a dime; if one worth a dollar doubles, one has made a dollar. And if one spends the dollar today, and waits to buy the dime stamp, by the time each has doubled in price he is ninety cents to the good.

The informed collector knows this; the neophyte collector in all probability does not have the practical good sense to realize it. The chances are that he is still beset with the "face-value syndrome" mentioned earlier, and to pay $5.00 for a stamp of three-cent denomination when one can buy a more recent three-cent stamp for a nickel is a gross display of philatelic ignorance. The informed collector knows which will prove to be the better buy.

Here again reference to the advertisements of leading dealers supplies a key. Does the reader ever recall having seen an advertisement of a dealer offering superb mint Columbians for sale, even of the lower values? While at one time or another such an ad may have appeared, at the moment such an incident does not come to mind. We have, however, seen no end of advertisements offering mint commemoratives of the past twenty or thirty years for sale, including the ten-cent Bell, which has proved to be such a useful stamp for purposes of comparison.

A dealer does not need to spend his advertising dollar offering for sale what he can sell with ease without advertising. Superb mint early commemoratives, in fact, anything in the earlier, better-grade, popular, and desirable issues of any country, of which the market supply is small, need never be advertised in order to sell them. The informed buyer seems possessed of an ability to ferret out such wanted merchandise, wherever and whenever it may be for sale. The advertisements are used more for offering for sale those competitive items, replacement of which is a simple matter, and for which the demand must be stimulated by one means or another.

The wise buyer can often assure that his dollars in any field are being spent more profitably by studying the size of the advertisements of dealers in that particular field.

Stamp advertising is expensive. Although there are a few big-city stamp shops that cater exclusively to local business, and hence find it unnecessary to advertise, by far the greater number of dealers who seek to do a national or even an international business devote a considerable part of their overhead expenses to advertising.

That money, as has been pointed out, is not going to be used to advertise stamps that can be sold without advertising.

The greater business that the dealer doing the advertising hopes to do, the more space he can devote to the advertisement. If he has a dozen of a certain item for sale, on which his profit is going to be small, it can only be advertised at minimum cost, if at all. On the other hand, if it is something that he has in large quantity, and if his markup on it is considerable, a large advertisement, even a full-page or a center-page display is justified.

It is not chance that finds the largest space users in our stamp magazines are the philatelic agents of the new nations, peddling their gaudy bits of paper, many of which never even saw a post office of the nation that issued them. The first-day-cover dealers, especially the manufacturers of cacheted envelopes, are regular full-page users. Scarcity of stock is not a problem with them, nor is replacement of merchandise sold. The publishers of albums and catalogues are also well represented, for they, too, are in the enviable position of pushing a button to increase supply to meet demand.

The dealer who has found that by studying the sheet of a new Israel issue he can detect a malformed letter on one stamp in each sheet can afford a huge advertisement calling attention to his discovery. The fact that every sheet of the stamp has the same "rare error" does not deter him from offering his "major variety" at an inflated price. (A two-inch ad, of course, wouldn't do the trick, for he is seeking the less-informed buyer, who naïvely believes that even if he can't afford the thousand-dollar rare errors, like the wealthy collectors, his "malformed S" in Israel will someday turn out to be as valuable.) If he collects long enough, he knows that the philatelic woods are full of "malformed S's," "rare" shades, "broken" frame lines, and misplaced vignettes, none of which will ever merit catalogue recognition, and none of which have any premium value, other than perhaps as an example of careless workmanship. (The twenty-four-cent air-mail invert, to be sure, is an example of careless workmanship, but it hardly can be compared with Israel's "malformed S"!)

The collector with a strong magnifying glass and equally strong eyes can have a field day with United States stamps. Anyone who understands printing and engraving processes knows that no two stamps can possibly be identical. Variations in the flow of ink into the tiny crevices in the plate will make for very visible varieties in the finished product. Interesting they may be, but they are of no value, although the first time the new collector comes upon a stamp with a portion uninked he is sure he has a rarity.

It is not within the province of this book to explain such philatelic terms as double transfers, misplaced entries, and inner frame lines. There is a wealth of philatelic literature available for those who seek to follow our fourth rule. Many of these varieties are listed in the Scott catalogue; many are priced over, some at quite substantial increases over, the normal price.

As a general rule, the purchase of minor varieties of this sort, even those of high values, will prove to be a rather poor investment. Most collectors interested in engraving varieties prefer to hunt for them themselves. This, too, is a means of finding that knowledge pays cash dividends. The relatively common three-cent 1851 in normal condition lists at seventy cents; if one finds this stamp with five lines recut in the triangle at the upper left, he has a stamp listing at $20.00. Not one collector in a thousand is even aware of what to look for to locate this variety; perhaps not one dealer in ten is even aware of its existence, and even fewer would know it when they saw it. A collector with even moderate knowledge of plate varieties on this stamp has the opportunity to pick up stamps listing at $20.00 and to buy them on the basis of a stamp listing at seventy cents.

And since the collector most interested in possessing plate varieties on the stamp selected for this discussion, the three-cent 1851, is the one who possesses the knowledge to pick them up at a very modest price, he seldom is a prospect to buy it on a basis of the higher price. It is precisely for this reason that collections of what some collectors call "flyspeck varieties" are often available at discounts from catalogue that would appear to be substantial. In fact, many times these very collections have been made up by the knowledgeable out of stamps bought as the ordinary, common varieties. When offered for sale, they provide the owner with a reward that well justifies the time he has devoted to seeking knowledge of his stamps.

There are other seeming incongruities in catalogue pricing which are only explainable in the light of market conditions.

A plate number block of six of the two-cent Hudson-Fulton, for example, lists at $50.00 when imperforate, but only $15.00 when perforated. On a comparative basis, the imperforate would appear to be three times scarcer than the perforated variety. In practice, the facts are quite the opposite. Auctions offer the imperforate block far more frequently than they do the perforated. Only the merest number of Hudson-Fulton imperforates were issued: 216,480, a handful compared to the 72,634,631 of the much more common perforated variety. But most of the imperforates were sold to philatelists, since very few post offices had them on sale; by far the bulk of the perforated stamps were sold to nonphilatelists and used up. The imperforate plate blocks are thus relatively scarce on the basis of the number that can exist, but relatively common in that most of those that do exist are in philatelic hands, and thus either on the market or hanging over the market. The perforated stamp, far more plentiful theoretically, and catalogued accordingly, is nevertheless far more difficult to find. A price of well over catalogue for a perfect example would be the rule rather than the exception; since condition is seldom a matter of relative importance on an imperforate stamp, it is not surprising that the more expensive block will bring a considerable discount from the catalogue price.

The collector who boasts that he never pays "more than half catalogue for any stamp" is actually paying tribute not to his astuteness in buying, but to his ignorance of the basic principles of stamp merchandising. While the chap who may boast that he only pays double catalogue may not necessarily have a better collection than his equally ignorant brother, yet if his buying has been wise and careful, if he has bought the right items and in the right condition, he conceivably could possess a collection that he could readily sell at a profit. Such is unlikely, of course, but nevertheless possible, especially if the collection were to consist of scarce, early popular material in the finest possible condition. It could not be the case were it made up of material freely available from almost any dealer.

Elementary though this may seem, it is a fact that many collectors find they cannot grasp. For there are many times in philately when catalogue price actually is the least relative factor in contemplating the purchase of a stamp.

About three years ago the stamp magazines commented on the sale price of a magnificently centered single of the two-cent Black Jack stamp, Scott #73, which bore a perfectly struck red cancel, showing a neat tiny flower. The stamp, the property of Howard Lehman, a collector whose ability to assess philatelic perfection is legendary in the stamp trade, brought more than two hundred dollars, despite its catalogue value of $5.00.

High as the price may have seemed at the time, it turned out to be a wonderful investment for the owner. Some two years later it again came on the market, but this time the price was in excess of seven hundred dollars; yet the catalogue price of the stamp had not increased in the meantime.

It was simply that the stamp was actually not one in a million, but perhaps even one in ten million. And the underbidder, as can readily be understood by any connoisseur of fine stamps, was none other than Howard Lehman, who found that as far as some stamps are concerned, the price is entirely a secondary matter. If this particular stamp ever comes up again, the realized price will be interesting to watch, especially in view of the fact that by now it has achieved an aura of desirability similar to that worn by the famous one-cent British Guiana of 1851.

There doesn't seem to be much question about it. It will never pay the wise collector to be a slave to the catalogue.

10. *Timing is a most important factor.* The late
Arthur Deas, an old-time collector and former president of the Collectors' Club of New York, once told the
writer an interesting story.

As a lad of about eighteen, Deas obtained a position with a
manufacturer of band instruments in lower New York. His
salary was a modest $6.00 per week, very little by today's stand-
ards, but enough to permit him to give something to his parents toward his keep and even leave a bit over to pursue his
stamp-collecting hobby.

One day Deas' employer received a letter from an Indiana
postmaster. The postmaster was also director of the band at the
local high school. While the band was returning from having
played at a neighboring school the train was wrecked. While
none of the passengers were injured, the baggage car at the
head of the train left the tracks and the band instruments
were shattered.

An adjustment with the insurance company was obtained,
and the postmaster was advised to place an order for new instruments. The year was 1893, and the set of stamps to commemorate the Chicago Columbian Exposition had just appeared.

The Indiana post office was a tiny one. The business that it
did in the course of a year was hardly sufficient to return its

142

postmaster enough income to provide a living, so he operated a general store as well. These mercantile activities, added to his postal duties, supplemented a very modest compensation for directing the school band. Thus he was afforded a sufficient income to maintain himself and his family.

Seventy years ago, as today, the compensation of a very small post office was exactly equal to the amount of business that it did in the course of a year. Even today there are thousands of these fourth-class post offices scattered throughout the nation. (Advocates of putting the post office on a "business basis" should contemplate this fact. A "business" would find it necessary to close up any "branches" which operated at a "deficit"; the post office rightly feels that a patron residing in a small town is as much deserving of postal service as one living in a large city.)

Of course there is a distinct limit to a postmaster's income on this basis. The moment his gross receipts exceed a given limit his post office automatically achieves higher status and his remuneration is calculated on an entirely different basis.

The Indiana postmaster saw an opportunity to pocket the insurance money simply by finding a musical-instrument manufacturer willing to take payment in postage stamps. The firm for which Deas worked was approached, but the deal was vetoed by the owner.

"But stamps are better than money," Deas remonstrated. "And especially now, with the Columbian stamps coming out, we'll have no trouble selling the stamps. As a matter of fact, if you will give me the discount you would give our regular salesman on the $800 order, I'll sell the stamps, and make a little extra for myself."

So sincere did the youngster seem that his boss accepted the order. The postmaster sent fifty sets of Columbians, all in very large blocks, with a face value of $817, and the instruments were sent. Deas devoted each lunch hour to calling on dealers to peddle the stamps. Each day he returned with varying sums of money which he turned over to his boss for credit to this account. Even if Deas had to accept a small discount from the face value of the stamps, it provided him with a small margin of profit because of the discount he had received on the sale of the instruments.

At length all of the values to the thirty-cent had been sold, but he still owed his boss a considerable sum of money. Some months later even the thirty-cent and fifty-cent stamps had been sold, at somewhat larger discounts. But there was no demand whatsoever for the dollar values.

Deas' salary by this time was a bit more than $6.00 per week, but he found himself working off what he still owed by permitting his employer to deduct part of the salary on each payday. It took a few years, but finally the entire indebtedness was paid off, and the stamps were his. But, to his dismay, there still was no sale for the stamps. Hundreds of others who had speculated in the Columbians found it rather sticky going when they tried to sell them. One could obtain a small premium for the dollar value, for a dealer in Elkhorn, Wisconsin, N. E. Carter, was trying to corner this one value on behalf of a wealthy collector, and he was buying up all he could find. Deas breathed a bit easier when the last of the dollar values was sold, but he still had more than six hundred dollars' face value in the two-, three-, four-, and five-dollar values.

About the turn of the century Arthur Deas married. When his father-in-law-to-be asked him what his prospects were, Deas mentioned his most outstanding asset, more than six hundred dollars in savings, but he failed to mention that the sum was in a comparatively unsalable commodity. The bride's father was apparently convinced, and the ceremony took place.

Periodically in the next few years Deas would trot the stamps around to the various dealers in the hope of getting face value from them. No longer was he willing to accept a discount, especially after having held them ten or twelve years. They didn't move.

In 1920 dealers were selling blocks of the higher values of the Columbians at retail at a discount from face value. A collector sufficiently affluent to spend $20.00 at a time for a block of the $5.00 Columbians was given a discount in exchange for his patronage. The stamp catalogued at $7.50 each, and the woods were full of collectors whose limit for a stamp—any stamp— was a third of Scott, and it mattered not one bit if this worked out to half face value, as it did.

Mrs. Deas at this point no doubt shared the original views of Deas' employer on the likelihood of making money through the purchase of postage stamps.

In the mid-1920s Deas had the opportunity to sell the entire remaining holding at face value. No longer was there an incentive to get his money back, for by now he was in his own business, making good money, and the matter of $600 was no longer the crucial concern that it had once been. Mrs. Deas remained singularly unimpressed. Shortly thereafter she died.

In the early 1930s Deas finally accepted an offer of three times the face value for the entire lot. In a few years what was worth less than six hundred dollars brought almost two thousand dollars. Sadly, he reflected that he would have given much more than the entire proceeds in order to make the final report not only to his wife, but to his former employer as well.

Today that $600 in face value would easily be worth close to $50,000, perhaps even more, for Deas recalled that there were many plate number blocks in the holding. But this fact even Deas was never to know, for he went to his own reward years before.

The story points its moral. Time and again philatelists point to the Columbian series of 1893 as an example of an investment in stamps that would have paid phenomenal returns to anyone fortunate enough to have bought them in 1893 and to have held them until 1960.

But the investor who held them from 1893, and then found it necessary to sell them in 1920, would question this. For he not only was denied any return on his "investment" for twenty-seven years, but when he finally did sell, he would receive much less than he had originally paid. For this man the Columbians were a decidedly poor investment.

Much more fortunate would be the investor who bought these in 1920, at a discount from face value, who in only forty years could sell them for a tremendous profit. A set of blocks of the entire issue which he could have bought without too much difficulty in 1920 for less than sixty dollars would bring from four to five thousand dollars forty years later.

The ability to look ahead is not given to us, so we cannot do more than guess what today's purchaser of a set of blocks at, let us say, $4,000 may contemplate getting for them at the close of this century. There are far too many imponderables involved, among them being the factor of inflation, and even the possibility of atomic elimination of the human race. A world populated by crabgrass and algae is not too likely to be a possible purchaser for a set of Columbian blocks.

Timing is a most important factor in establishing whether a philatelic purchase is destined to be a profitable one or not. The time of purchase is fully as important as the time chosen to sell. One cannot say that the purchase of Columbians was a wise move, or a sad one, without ascertaining when the purchase was made and when the sale was contemplated.

There are not many large holdings of Columbians existing today. Perhaps the sole remaining one turned up in England but a few years ago, when a large quantity of them, including part sheets of the dollar values, came up for auction in a single lot. An American collector ill in Britain had rewarded his attentive nurse with a neatly tied bundle, advising her to hold it until she needed the money, and then to offer it for sale. The bundle, when sold, brought more than forty thousand dollars.

One frequently encounters rumors of the existence of sets of the Columbians in complete sheets. There is scarcely a dealer who cannot repeat the tale of the chap who has come to him with the solemn disclosure that he knows of someone possessing such a valuable holding. Some fifteen years ago Ezra D. Cole, the Nyack, New York, dealer decided to set these rumors at rest for all time. In an advertisement in a leading stamp magazine he offered to pay $1,000 to anyone who could just *show* him a complete sheet of the five-dollar Columbian. No one has ever shown up to collect the reward.

But tale-tellers die hard. Some time in the next few months we will be approached, as will many other philatelists, by someone who will assure us, for whatever use we want to put the information, that he knows someone who has a complete sheet of the $5.00 Columbian.

Timing in selling at the right time is a factor in other ways.

The Scott catalogue fortunately is not a static thing. As information about various stamps is definitely established, listings are withdrawn or, in some cases, added. Generally the debate on the status of a disputed stamp or issue waxes hot. Those possessing examples of it, and dealers who have made many sales of the item, are most insistent that the listing be retained; those whose beliefs are not tinged with such self-interest are just as vehement that the item be delisted.

Generally changes in the catalogue are foreshadowed by discussions in the philatelic magazines. (Just how anyone can feel that he can collect intelligently without being a subscriber to at least the three or four leading stamp publications is something which we have never been able to understand.)

When the United States Navy incorporated ships of the French navy into its fleet in North Africa in 1944, it had the problem of supplying stamps to the French sailors for their mail. If ordinary United States stamps were supplied, the French could easily convert these into money by discounting them among American servicemen. To make this impossible, United States air-mail stamps were surcharged "R.F." (République Française) for use on letters sent by the French sailors. The stamps were listed in the Scott catalogue, and proved immensely popular. Some of them brought fairly substantial sums when their relative rarity was ascertained.

However, competent research by a student of our air-mail stamps, Henry Goodkind of New York, established that the stamps in mint condition actually had no philatelic standing, since their proper use required that they be affixed to letters at the time of posting, and that philatelic desirability extended to them only when properly used, and when used by those authorized to use them. The next issue of the catalogue listed them only in used condition; additionally, the market differentiates between legitimate military use and philatelic use. Many philatelists at the time put them on unaddressed envelopes, and obliging French mail clerks supplied routine postmarks and even censorship seals.

Delisting of the stamps brought such a release of supplies that one still finds them listed in almost every auction. Whereas they had been earlier thought to be relatively scarce, the haste to unload has shown how plentiful they actually were, and it has in addition cast doubt on the authenticity of many of the surcharges. In this case, the additional supplies, coupled with the cloud under which the stamps were sold, brought about a collapse in price. Timing was indeed a consideration in the sale of these stamps.

For many years the Scott catalogue carried a listing for a United States postal card listed as No. UX 34. This was a one-cent postal card on which a surcharge reading "1 Cent" had been placed. Since the card was already of the one-cent denomination, the surcharge was rather redundant and unnecessary, and it was regarded as an error. For many years there were persistent rumors that far from being an error, the card was actually a deliberately prepared affair, brought about when a philatelist bribed a postal clerk to run a quantity of the cards through the surcharge machine which was intended to render unused two-cent cards into one-cent cards, when the rate was reduced.

The card is now in process of being eliminated from the catalogue. Listed at $27.50 in one edition, it was dropped to $15.00 in the next; its next price will be $7.50, after which it will be deleted altogether. Just as the veterinarian thought it less painful to cut the dog's tail off a half inch at a time, instead of in one operation, so the catalogue publishers feel that a steadily-declining price should give those with specimens of the card ample warning that their value is diminishing. It is surprising how many examples of a card once thought to be rare are now appearing. The timing on this item has a great deal to do with the price at which one will be able to sell it.

When World War II broke out, the pound sterling had a value in our money of $4.03. A short time later, as German successes and British revenues brought about a flight from sterling, the pound sank to under three dollars. (It has never recovered; today it has been stabilized at $2.80.)

British Colonial stamps, always one of the most popular of collecting fields, suffered greatly from the devaluation. British dealers, selling for dollars, could now cut their price by one-third and still obtain as much for their stamps as they had obtained before the devaluation. The face value of every British and Colonial stamp and set overnight was reduced by one-third. Rare commemorative sets which for years had an established value tumbled in price as British dealers, heeding their nation's call for added dollars, sought to take advantage of the devaluation. The 1935 Jubilees, which dealers had shortly before offered to buy at $90.00, became freely available at $75.00; the 1937 Coronations had their boom abortively shortened, and dropped far below face value, a level at which they are still available today.

In time prices leveled off, and dealers on both sides of the Atlantic adjusted to the new figures. But timing in both buying and selling was a most important factor to those collectors and dealers who were caught by the overnight drop in sterling. Prime beneficiaries, of course, were British dealers and collectors, for while the cash in their pockets, the money in their banks, and their savings and insurance may have suffered with the devaluation, their stamps retained their previous value in terms of outside currencies.

Time has a philatelic consideration in yet another sense: the time that a dealer considering the purchase of a collection is able to give it for purposes of examination and determination of value.

Granted that virtually every collection ever assembled will someday be put up for sale, and granted that when that day does come the then owner wants to realize the best possible price for it, it would seem that the title for these few words should interest most readers.

The truth of the second aphorism is self-evident. We've met all sorts of collectors and dealers in our time, but we don't ever expect to meet one who wants less for his stamps than they are worth. Most often it is the other way round.

What surprises most professionals is that while collectors naturally want the highest price possible for their stamps, too often they will not lift a finger to make a high price possible. Whether this is motivated by laziness or some other attribute we decline to pass judgment, but that the situation exists is undeniable.

The most important rule in preparing a collection for sale is to have it in such manner that it can be inspected—and as long as the backs of stamps are as important as the fronts (in order to determine condition) this means that the entire stamp must be visible and subject to examination.

Transparent stamp pockets (sometimes known as pochettes) may serve their purpose in protecting stamps against possible damage, or in preserving the gum. We emphasize the word "may," because sometimes the very device intended to preserve a stamp may be the actual device that contributes to its destruction. However, when a collection is to be sold, the mounts have performed their mission, and should be discarded.

Like every other dealer, our own extensive collection of burned fingers (ten, at last count!) causes us to shy away from collections done up in pochettes. Even if the owner is sincere that "every stamp is perfect," the fact still remains that he may have bought a repaired or a regummed stamp in all good faith.

Taking a "spot check" is no protection, except, possibly, to establish a percentile of stamps that are not in the condition they are represented to be. Deducting a certain sum from the total may serve to protect the buyer, but it is not fair to the seller in the event that the "check" disclosed fewer "cripples" than the ratio seemed to indicate. For that reason, to bring a fair figure, a collection in pochettes should be stripped of its outer garments and put in a stock book where the prospective purchaser can examine the stamps, front and back, with comparative ease and a minimum of investment in time. Nudity in a stamp collection, far from being a cause for shame, is the finest assurance there is that every stamp will bring its full value.

Another common failing of the collector attempting to sell his stamps is the gosh-awful mess of cheap and worthless debris that surrounds his choice gems. We have been offered collections that came in the most varied assortment imaginable of cigar boxes, pill cans, pliofilm bags from the dry cleaner, cornflakes containers, and even, once, a thermos bottle. If all of the contents were worthless, it would present little or no problem, but sometimes such items were jammed into these containers years ago. At that time a Pony Express plate block may have been no more valuable than a plate block of a commemorative that may have appeared ten years earlier; today it is a different matter.

If the seller of the stamps considers his time too valuable to spend the required effort to render his stamps salable, what obligation does the buyer have to agree that his time is even less valuable? We would suggest that none at all, unless of course the seller is willing to compensate him for the investment by accepting a lower price.

An investment of even a few hours in sorting out the inevitable cigar boxes will pay substantial dividends. By placing the better, more valuable items in a stock book where they can be seen, examined, and figured individually, the owner will be assured of a better price for the items. And the statement from the seller, "The better items are in this book; everything in the cigar boxes is more or less common," will establish a better buyer-seller relationship at the very beginning than does the usual approach, "Here's ten cigar boxes containing some really wonderful stamps." With that gambit, all the prospective purchaser will see when he looks is the skim milk, not the cream.

If the stamps are offered in such manner that they can be

examined, it will not take long for the buyer to establish what he feels to be a fair price. Getting him to disclose this price is in all likelihood not going to be an easy matter, unless (as sometimes happens) the seller has complete confidence in the prospective buyer's honesty. (It is by no means unusual in the stamp trade, where the majority of collectors and dealers are fair in their dealings, for the party to the transaction to accept the other's price without question—when there is a basis for complete confidence.)

In our experience, and this goes back quite a few years, we have yet to meet the owner of a stamp collection who does not have a very good idea of what he wants for it. He may be reluctant to admit this fact. In fact, he usually is, for the same reason that the buyer is reluctant to show his hand first by stating the price that he has come to in figuring it. It is at this point that tempers flare and words can sometimes become harsh. The owner who hasn't "the slightest idea of what the collection is worth" suddenly becomes possessed of uncanny philatelic ability when an offer is submitted. Whereas a moment ago no one had seen the collection, he suddenly recalls that three people had offered him more. Minutes before, when he was asked what the collection had cost him, or what he felt it was worth, a blank stare was the only reply. Now, suddenly, the figures as to catalogue value, retail value, replacement cost, and comparative offerings pour out.

We draw the curtain at this point. Each party to the transaction is on his own. As long as the buyer and seller each know the point at which a meeting of the minds will occur, there is every likelihood that business will result. If, however, the prospective buyer is insistent on buying the collection for less than he should, or if the seller holds out for too high a price, the protagonists must, of necessity, break off the battle, to have it resumed another day, with perhaps some changes in the cast of characters.

A few more suggestions might be in order at this point, even though they bear little reference to this final rule.

The philatelist who is proud of his hobby will let all know of his interest at every opportunity. While it might be somewhat boastful to brag of the value of his collection (as well as unwise, the frequency of stamp robberies being what they are), he should let no opportunity pass in casual conversation, in newspaper interviews, in hobby discussions. One never knows when something in the stamp line might turn up right in one's own back yard, and the opportunity to share in what might be a find or an advantageous purchase may be greatly enhanced.

No longer does the admission that one is a stamp collector expose him to ridicule. This is the day when any hobby, no matter how bizarre, is respected. But it must be admitted that to many people even philately is a bizarre pursuit.

We had a phone call one night from a dealer who had not long before sold us a set of new tires for our car. During the transaction he had chanced to ask our vocation, and our reply left him momentarily tongue-tied, as is often the case, but he soon recovered his vocal equilibrium, and we thought no more of the incident.

One evening, some weeks later, the telephone rang. It was our tire dealer.

"How about coming over?" he asked. "We have a guest here who collects stamps, and you really ought to know each other."

Philately may be a common interest to many folk, but the opportunity to meet a new philatelist is hardly an event that is calculated to make one change whatever plans he may have had for any particular evening.

"Thanks for thinking of it," we replied, "but why do you think this would be such a treat?"

154

"Well, you're both stamp collectors," he replied.

"Thanks a lot," we ventured. "You know, about a month ago I had a customer here who is in the tire business. It never occurred to me to ask you over."

"Why should it have?" our caller asked. To this day we are certain that he doesn't understand at all the reason for our remark. To the uninitiated the philatelist is a breed apart, and the fact that we did not hasten to drop whatever we were doing at that moment to meet a fellow philatelist is something our tire-dealer friend could probably never comprehend.

We recall a good friend in England who is very much interested in picture postcards. He has found that among seemingly common lots of these there can be better-than-ordinary stamps, special postmarks, and even unusual views for which there is a rather steady demand. He has been advertising in various weekly publications for them, offering to pay five shillings per hundred for all that are sent him. The result is a rather slow but steady flow, but hardly enough to do much more than cover the cost of the advertisements.

He tried the same ad in a monthly magazine published by the church of which he was an adherent. The results were no better and no worse than they had been in other media. And then the bright flash struck.

The new advertisement read:

SEND ME ONE HUNDRED PICTURE POSTCARDS AND I WILL DONATE FIVE SHILLINGS TO WHICHEVER CHURCH YOU DESIGNATE.

His name and address followed.

Within two weeks the flow of cards started, and as he places the ads in other religious magazines, the flow has been stimulated. Readers who apparently wouldn't be bothered to make a shipment for five shillings hastened to do it when the opportunity to do something for their church became the greater objective.

"Good show," we remarked to our friend. "You're the only one I've ever heard of who used divine worship to build a stamp collection!"

There are some further observations that should be known about in order to make the road to philatelic profits an easier one to follow.

When you are on to something good, don't share knowledge of it with too many people.

When collectors discovered that plate number 25365 on the one-and-one-half cent Mount Vernon stamp was a relatively scarce number, the news was given to the philatelic press, and from one end of the nation to the other collectors flocked to post offices to seek the elusive number. So many were found that even though it actually was scarce in the standpoint of impressions made from that plate, every possible prospect for it, instead, became a potential seller, and what might have been a scarce item turned out to be common.

When a dealer turned up a sheet of the sixteen-cent air-mail special delivery completely lacking vertical perforations, back in the late 1930s, he bought the sheet, and sealed his lips for a ten-year period. Whether others existed in post offices, waiting to be sold to those seeking them, will never be known, but since the existence of the sheet was not divulged until years later, the fortunate owner was certain that he had the only one in existence. Today it catalogues at $1,750 per pair. Had others been found, the value of his own find would have been considerably reduced.

The dealer who chanced to find a two-cent Harding Memorial stamp printed by the rotary-press process but perforated eleven knew that he had made an astounding discovery, but he kept the news to himself. Instead of rushing into print with news of his find, he started to buy quantities of the Harding stamps in used condition, stamps that were so common that a dollar would buy 300 of them. For a period of years, until he believed that he had cleaned out the wholesale market, no one knew the reason for his interest.

When he made the announcement of the existence of Scott #613 he had found more than a dozen examples of what is today the rarest of all United States commemorative stamps. The Scott catalogue price in the 1962 catalogue is $1,500—rather a tidy return on his investment of a paltry few hundred dollars.

The writer has examined a complete sheet of one of our 1959 commemoratives, the possession of a Colorado collector, issued with vertical perforations lacking. Our advice to him was to withhold any mention of it for at least ten years. Premature news of the existence of the SEATO part perforate stamp, Scott #1151, stimulated a rush to post offices to locate supplies. They were found in offices as scattered and far apart as South Dakota and New York. Careful concealment of the secret might have permitted the original finders a far better reward for their find.

A further observation is offered to those who hasten to climb aboard an issue of a provisional printing.

Often temporary shortage of a single value in a set of foreign stamps will create a situation where the solution is the surcharging of another value, to create the denomination required. During the last war, when ordinary shipping routes were difficult to maintain, this occurred frequently among many British colonies. Bermuda, Bahamas, Ceylon, and Newfoundland all came out with issues of low face value, which were on sale for only limited periods, until additional supplies of the denomination in question could be obtained from the Crown agents in London.

Caution is always advised when purchase of a stamp of very low face value at a price well in excess of face value is considered. We can think of few instances where the prices at which these "rare" provisionals were originally available have "held." Rather, opportunists on the spot in each instance have bought virtually the entire supply, and unloading them at many times face value, at the same time feeding stamp magazines with stories of their alleged scarcity, have been able to clean up. If one doubts this, we know of one dealer in Bermuda who made enough on one provisional stamp issued in that island in 1946 to enable him to buy a very comfortable villa.

It pays to remember that the greater the margin of profit the buyer gives the seller, the less likely he is to make a profit when it comes his turn to sell.

One final bit of advice that may be the most valuable suggestion made in this entire book: when you have found a dealer in whose sagacity, honesty, sincerity, and fairness you have no doubt, treasure that friendship like no other. Share your custom with other dealers, should you so desire, but let your relationship with your trusted dealer be one that you may always be proud of.

The medical profession has its crooked doctors, the legal profession its shyster lawyers. Such individuals are rare indeed, and what success these pariahs may have comes only when their dealings are with those unable or unwilling to patronize the legitimate practitioners. Philately, too, has its pariahs, and, happily, they, too, are in the distinct minority. Were it not for the fact that in philately, as in every other field, there are those who believe that quality, reputation, and honesty are not an integral part of every transaction, such individuals would not exist to cause concern.

POSTSCRIPT

Almost exactly one hundred years ago the first catalogue of postage stamps appeared. An Englishman, Dr. Gray, in a pocket-size book, made a listing of all of the known stamps that had appeared up to 1862. Most of them were illustrated with sketches.

The catalogue did not carry any prices, nor did it attempt to cover the aspect of relative value. Value was of no concern to the collectors of a century ago. Dealers had not yet come upon the scene, and stamp collecting was one of many pleasant hobbies, embarked upon only as a method of making an otherwise drab, monotonous, or even tedious life pass more enjoyably.

Dr. Gray in his foreword, with a glance into the future, indulged in a bit of phophecy.

"There is every prospect that in years to come the collecting of stamps may grow in importance. There is even a chance that someday it will be so widely followed that the number of people interested in stamps will exceed the number that now collect such popular items as feathers and even birds' eggs."

Dr. Gray, of course, never realized that his prophecy was to come true to a greater extent than his wildest dreams could foresee. Within five years of the appearance of his first catalogue, priced catalogues were regularly appearing; within ten years enterprising men, and women, too, were earning their livings from the sale of stamps. Within fifteen years stamp auctions were being held, and regularly published stamp magazines were appearing. Stamp organizations, some of them still in existence today, were meeting regularly.

The number of philatelic books that have appeared in the past hundred years, from the Dr. Gray catalogue to this one, is a substantial one. It is doubtful whether anyone could ever ascertain just how many there are. They run the gamut from a light-hearted, gay book of philatelic cartoons called *All in Fun* (Lucius Jackson) to one with the rather terrifying title of *Distinguishing Characteristics of Old German Stamps* (Herman Schloss).

Somewhere between these two extremes the reader will find this book. It is the author's hope that some of the tales told herein will bring the chuckle, the smile, and the pleasant recollection that the Jackson book brought to so many; it is our hope, as well, that the practical aspects of the book, the suggestions, the tips, and the advice will prove to be as beneficial to the stamp buyer as the information contained in the Schloss book.

When our earlier book, *Nassau Street,* was in manuscript form, our son Kenneth, then in high school, was told by his English teacher that some time during the school year he would have to read a book, in order to write a report on it. Kenneth's indifference to things philatelic is perhaps exceeded only by a dislike for the printed word, especially when it is bound between two hard covers.

"My dad is writing a book," he reported to the teacher, "and I'm sure he is going to make me read it. Can I use that for the report?"

"Absolutely not," was the reply. "This has to be a regularly published book, one that you can find in a library."

Kenneth returned home crestfallen, unhappy at the prospect of being required to read two books that term, not one. We hastened to explain that he should tell the teacher that *Nassau Street* was indeed to be a regularly published book, and that it could conceivably happen that the Lakeland High School library might even eventually have one on its shelves.

The teacher relented when this was made clear, and one evening, between television programs, Kenneth retired to his room with the manuscript. One hour later he took his place before the evidence of man's genius known as the "idiot box," handing the finished book report to his father.

Nassau Street [it began] is a book about stamps that tells of the tough times my father had in his early days. It has a lot of stories in it, some of which I enjoyed. Much of it isn't very interesting, but it ends happily because my father became successful in the end.

When the television program gave way to a lengthy commercial, we engaged Kenneth in conversation.

No, he hadn't read the introduction. Introductions never say anything anyway. In English he learned that all they are to do is to get the reader ready for the main story. The conclusion? No, that just sums up what the book was about, and usually repeats everything already said.

"What parts did you read in the half-hour you gave it?" we asked.

"Oh, I turned to the middle. The beginning didn't seem important, and I found out all I needed for the report from the middle, so I didn't have to read the end."

A prophet is generally without honor in his own country, and a parent certainly is without too much esteem in the eyes of his teen-age children. We all know of the wag who reported that he knew, when he was seventeen or eighteen, that his father was a dope, but what amazed him was how much the old man learned in the next five or six years.

We would not wish any of our readers to be called upon to

give a book report on this volume. But if such should happen, we do hope that somewhat greater attention is paid to these pages than Kenneth gave to *Nassau Street*.

As promised in our introduction (who reads introductions, anyhow?), this has not been a book titled "How to Make Money in Stamps."

It is our hope, however, that our assurance made in the earlier pages will be borne out.

This book will not tell anyone how to make money in stamps, but it will be difficult for anyone reading it and profiting by its advice, suggestions, and help, to lose money on his "investment." If careful attention is paid to the remarks contained between these two covers, the reader will find out what was meant when someone once said, "Let us give thanks for philately; it is the only hobby in the world in which a man can eat his cake and have it too."

With the help of this book, it is our sincere desire that all who have read it will find this tribute will come true.

MARKET GUIDE

As an aid to collectors and dealers who read this book, we are glad to append our impressions of the stamp market at the time of the book's appearance. In keeping with our continued suggestion that it is supply and demand which determine the marketability of stamps, and therefore, the price as well, two columns are given in each case, one giving the supply, and the other the demand.

Readers will find that their most profitable purchases will be in those categories in which the supply is small and the demand great. Since fashions and fads develop in stamps, just as in other fields, this information is most true at the present moment; it may not be as true five or ten years from now.

Philatelists seeking an interesting field to collect in which fun is the primary consideration are advised to consider those categories in which the supply is large, and the demand limited. Buying opportunities in these fields should be far better than in the others, and there should be possibilities for building up a substantial collection at most moderate cost, which might well have possibilities for profit at a later date.

One final caution is in order: the prospective buyer of stamps is strongly advised to avoid the seeking of bargain prices in those items on which demand is strong and supply is weak. Such bargains only exist when the seller is completely unaware of the identity or the value of the stamp or stamps. No knowledgeable seller will offer a bargain on an item that he can sell with ease at a substantial price.

Since condition is the all-important factor of market price (as quoted often in the Scott catalogue), each category is further broken down into three grades of condition:

"GEMS—Something prized for beauty, perfection, etc.," (Webster)

"CHOICE—That which is preferable." (Webster)

"STANDARD—That which is established by authority, custom or general consent as a model or example." (Webster) *

The word "standard" requires explanation. It refers to the condition of the vast majority of stamps on the market at any given moment, i.e., stamps reasonably attractive, undamaged, in short, a copy which, while not perfect, is what informed collectors would call "fine." If the stamp is unused, it may have either part or no gum; if used, the cancellation is not too heavy. This is the classification which perhaps 75 per cent of all philatelic transactions embrace.

United States Stamps	Supply	Demand
Postage issues, nineteenth century, unused		
Gems	Miniscule	Very strong
Choice	Small	Very strong
Standard	Moderate	Strong
Postage issues, nineteenth century, used		
Gems	Very small	Very strong
Choice	Small	Very strong
Standard	Moderate	Strong

---

* We are indebted to the late Hugh M. Clark for these definitions, which were used by him in an article written in 1944.

United States Stamps	Supply	Demand
Postage issues, nineteenth century, on cover		
Gems, if rare	Miniscule	Very strong
Choice, if rare	Small	Very strong
Standard, ordinary run	Small	Strong
Postage issues, twentieth century, unused		
Gems	Miniscule	Very strong
Choice	Very small	Very strong
Standard	Very small	Very strong
Postage issues, twentieth century, used		
Gems	Small	Very strong
Choice	Small	Strong
Standard	Small	Strong
Commemoratives, pre-1926, unused and used		
Gems	Exceedingly small	Very strong
Choice	Small	Very strong
Standard	Small	Strong
Commemoratives, post-1925, unused		
Gems	Moderate	Very strong
Choice	Adequate	Good
Standard	Plentiful	Good
First-day covers		
Pre-1928	Small	Very strong
1928 to date	Ample	Good
Airpost issues		
Pre-1934	Small	Very strong
1935 to date	Ample	Strong
Booklet panes, all	Small	Strong
Special delivery issues, pre-1917		
Gems	Miniscule	Very strong
Choice	Very small	Very strong
Standard	Small	Strong
Special delivery issues, 1917 to date	Good	Good
Official stamps, used and unused		
Gems	Miniscule	Very strong
Choice	Small	Good
Standard	Ample	Limited

United States Stamps	Supply	Demand
Newspapers and periodicals	Small	Limited
Parcel-post issues	Good	Good
Carriers and locals *		
Gems	Miniscule	Very strong
Choice	Small	Strong
Standard	Moderate	Fair
Envelopes and cut squares	Good	Good
Postal cards		
Mint	Very small	Very strong
Used	Small	Strong
Proof or essay form	Very small	Very strong
Revenue and fiscal stamps, pre-1871		
Gems	Very small	Very strong
Choice	Small	Strong
Standard	Ample	Good
Revenue and fiscal stamps, 1871 to 1930s	Ample	Good
Documentaries, stock transfers, 1940 to date	Plentiful	Limited
Private proprietary revenue stamps	Small	Strong
Proofs and essays	Miniscule	Very strong
Encased postage stamps	Miniscule	Strong
Postage currency	Very small	Strong
Telegraph stamps	Very small	Limited
Christmas seals		
Pre-1914	Good	Good
1914 to date	Plentiful	Very limited
Confederate states stamps, on or off cover		
Gems	Miniscule	Very strong
Choice	Very small	Very strong
Standard	Small	Very strong
United States possessions		
Philippine Islands	Ample	Fair

* It is understood that these items would be authenticated as genuine and accompanied by suitable guarantees. Most of these encountered in old collections are reprints, remainders, or outright counterfeits, for which there is very little demand.

166

Market Guide

United States Stamps	Supply	Demand
United States possessions (cont.)		
Canal Zone	Good	Strong
Hawaii	Small	Strong
Guam and U.S. Cuba occupation	Small	Modest
Puerto Rico	Small	Strong
Ryukyus, under U.S. mandate	Good	Good
Danish West Indies	Small	Good
United States mint sheets		
Pre-1928	Small	Very strong
1929-1932	Moderate	Very strong
1933 to date	Ample	Good
Souvenir sheets		
Mint	Good	Very strong
Used	Small	Good
Vending and affixing machine stamps (private perforations)	Small	Good

Foreign Stamps	Supply	Demand
BRITISH COMMONWEALTH		
Great Britain	Good	Strong
Australia	Small	Very strong
British West Indies	Good	Good
Burma	Ample	Weak
Canada	Small	Very strong
Egypt	Ample	Weak
Ghana	Ample	Weak
India	Good	Weak
Newfoundland	Small	Strong
New Zealand	Small	Good
South Africa	Good	Weak
Newly emerged African nations	Ample	Weak
OTHER COUNTRIES		
Afghanistan	Fair	Weak
Albania	Fair	Weak
Austria	Good	Good
Bavaria	Good	Fair
Belgium	Good	Strong
Bulgaria	Small	Weak

Foreign Stamps	Supply	Demand
OTHER COUNTRIES (cont.)		
China		
Empire, Pre-1912	Small	Strong
Republic	Good	Good
*People's Republic	Ample	Negligible
*Czechoslovakia	Ample	Fair
Danzig	Good	Good
Denmark	Good	Good
Finland	Good	Good
France	Ample	Good
Germany		
Empire	Moderate	Strong
1918 to date	Ample	Good
Greece	Good	Weak
*Hungary	Ample	Weak
Iceland	Small	Strong
Israel	Ample	Strong
Italy	Good	Good
Japan	Good	Strong
Jugoslavia	Good	Good
Korea	Small	Weak
*Liberia	Ample	Weak
Liechtenstein	Good	Strong
Luxembourg	Good	Strong
Manchukuo	Small	Weak
Monaco	Good	Good
Netherlands and colonies	Good	Good
Norway	Small	Good
Persia (Iran)	Small	Small
Philippines		
Pre-1945	Small	Fair
1945 to date	Ample	Weak
*Poland	Moderate	Good
Portugal	Good	Weak
*Romania	Ample	Weak
*Russia	Ample	Fair

* Countries with an asterisk preceding the name have flooded the market with used stamps which have actually been cancelled to order. Such stamps are generally regarded with disdain by knowledgeable collectors, and though cheap, their resale value is negligible.

Foreign Stamps	Supply	Demand
OTHER COUNTRIES (cont.)		
Saar	Good	Good
San Marino	Good	Good
Spain	Good	Good
Sweden	Good	Strong
Switzerland	Good	Strong
Turkey	Good	Weak
Vatican City	Ample	Fair
LATIN AMERICA		
Argentine Republic	Good	Fair
Bolivia	Good	Fair
Brazil	Good	Good
Chile	Good	Good
Colombia	Good	Fair
Costa Rica	Good	Strong
Cuba		
Pre-Castro	Good	Strong
Post-Castro	Presently illegal to possess	
Ecuador	Good	Fair
Guatemala	Good	Strong
Honduras	Good	Weak
Mexico	Good	Strong
Nicaragua	Good	Weak
Panama	Good	Moderate
Paraguay	Ample	Weak
Peru	Good	Good
Salvador	Good	Weak
Uruguay	Good	Fair
Venezuela	Good	Good